EARLY SOUTHERN TOWNS

Everett B. Wilson

EARLY SOUTHERN TOWNS

CASTLE BOOKS ★ NEW YORK

This edition published by arrangement with
A. S. BARNES AND CO., INC.

Printed in the United States of America

Dedication

*To: Chuck, Jac, and John
—longtime southern friends
who helped with this book*

Foreword

OLDER HOMES AND OTHER EARLY BUILDINGS in or near 48 early southern towns are described and pictured in this book, which rounds out a theme developed in other works by the author—*America East* and *Fifty Early American Towns*. All of the buildings presented are believed to have been built or started before 1860 and hence are more than 100 years old.

The brief early histories of the 48 towns do not report developments occuring later than about 100 years ago.

The book takes the reader into nine states south of the Potomac River and east of the Mississippi River, although Louisiana, of course, lies both east and west of that river. Florida is not included, because its one early town—St. Augustine, the oldest of all—was dealt with rather fully in *America East*. That volume also devoted considerable attention to Charleston, Savannah, and the James River area in Virginia, so they are not included. Certain parts of the nine states are missing because of space limitations.

In general, the nine states are presented in geographical order; that is, from north to south and east to west. So are the towns within the states and the buildings located in or near the towns.

Buildings described as being "open" are not all museums. Some are churches in regular use, and some are older houses that have been converted into commercial establishments or public buildings to which the public has access.

There is considerable disagreement about when some of the buildings were constructed or started, and in many cases the dates given are estimates. Where differences of opinion have been encountered, the author has tried to adopt the date most recently advanced, on the theory that it probably is based on later evidence. Many of the dates are approximate, whether or not it is so stated.

Garden clubs, historical societies, chambers of commerce, and authors of earlier books have been helpful sources of much of the factual information presented here.

By far the greatest amount of useful data on dates, locations, architectural details, and interior finish and decoration has been taken from the State Guides compiled in the Writers' Program conducted by the Work Projects (or Works Progress) Administration and sponsored by state and local governments and agencies.

Recent population figures refer to the 1960 census.

With the exceptions noted in the acknowledgements, the photographs were taken by the author.

E.B.W.

Bethesda, Maryland

Acknowledgments

THE AUTHOR IS GREATLY INDEBTED TO THE owners of the various houses and buildings that he was privileged to photograph, and to numerous local groups that provided maps and other helpful information.

He is most appreciative of the photographs of the Gorgas House and the President's Mansion loaned by the Greater Tuscaloosa Chamber of Commerce and is greatly indebted to Mr. and Mrs. Robert Warner, Washington, Connecticut, who very ably and kindly provided the photographs of Beaufort.

Special assistance was received from the Historical Societies of Leesburg, New Bern, Beaufort, and Harrodsburg.

Pamphlets issued annually by the Garden Club of Virginia were most helpful in identifying, locating, and describing historic buildings in that state.

Mr. and Mrs. C. W. Orttenburger, Richmond; the DeHardit Press, Gloucester; the Public Libraries of Fairfax and Warrenton; Mrs. Alden Kelly, Gallatin, and the Gulf Graphic, Ocean Springs (Natchez) Mississippi, contributed substantially to the histories of those towns.

In addition, valued assistance was received from:

Mrs. Paul Burnam, Richmond.

Mr. and Mrs. Jac M. Carpenter, Cincinnati, Ohio.

Mr. and Mrs. John M. Caffery, Jr., Westwego, Louisiana.

Mr. John G. Lewis, Hamilton, Virginia.

Mrs. Richard E. Robbins, Alexandria, Louisiana.

Mrs. Soaper Caffery, Harrodsburg.

Mrs. Judy Miller, office of Representative W. R. Anderson, of Tennessee, Washington, D.C.

Contents

EARLY SOUTHERN TOWNS

Early Building in the South

IT HAS BEEN WIDELY RECOGNIZED THAT the state of Virginia has many fine old homes and that such venerable southern cities as Charleston, Savannah, Natchez, and New Orleans can proudly point to numerous old dwellings of great appeal. What has not been so generally realized is that each of the nine southern states with which this book is concerned has a considerable number of buildings that possess genuine charm, architectural importance, or historical significance.

The largest numbers of towns and cities still having a noteworthy supply of early structures are to be found in Virginia and Kentucky. North Carolina and Mississippi are not too far behind. The fewest old communities with important numbers of early houses are found in South Carolina and Louisiana, but what those states do have are sufficiently attractive to make up for any difference in sheer numbers.

In the South, not too many early towns have remained small through the years. For example, Alexandria (Virginia), Raleigh, Columbia (South Carolina), Macon, Lexington, Louisville, Knoxville, Nashville, Huntsville, Montgomery, and New Orleans have grown considerably, to the point where they should not be described as towns today.

Others have remained surprisingly small. Three, in fact—Gloucester in Virginia, Halifax in North Carolina, and Shakertown in Kentucky—still have fewer than 1000 people. No more than 5000 persons are to be found in Berryville, Leesburg, and Warrenton, Virginia; Edenton, North Carolina; Washington, Georgia; Bardstown, Kentucky, and Port Gibson, Mississippi. A half dozen others covered in this book remain well under 10,000 in population.

As is true to the north, these southern states also have their quaint old towns, notably Halifax, Shakertown, and Natchitoches in Louisiana, which are a delight to the visitor after experiencing the rigors of high-speed travel over interstate highways and the perplexities of big city traffic.

The oldest of the 48 towns are found, for the most part, on or close to the East Coast and Gulf Coast. Settled first, in 1670, was Alexandria (Virginia). New Bern and Beaufort came, next in 1710, and Edenton followed in 1714. Exceptions inland are Columbia (South Carolina) first settled around 1700, Warrenton settled in 1712, and Natchitoches, settled in 1714, some four years ahead of New Orleans.

Tuscaloosa did not get its first white settlers until 1816, and Selma not until 1817. The other towns in the book were settled in between the extremes that have been mentioned. All but nine of the towns were settled or founded before 1800. While settlement in the south came later, on the average, than in the north, 22 of these early towns are more than 200 years old and all are at least 150 years old.

Substantial old sections are to be found in a number of the communities, notably Alexandria (Virginia), Fredericksburg, Chapel Hill, Salisbury, Edenton, New Bern, Augusta, Athens, Washington, Milledgeville, Lexington, Harrodsburg, Frankfort, Huntsville, and Natchez, not to mention New Orleans with its picturesque and unspoiled Vieux Carre or French Quarter.

In all of the communities just named, the old buildings are numerous enough and close enough together to give one the feeling of an early town, even though in many cases new buildings have been interspersed with the old. The one exception is Shakertown, which became a virtual ghost town earlier in this century, but now is being restored under the Federal urban renewal program.

Despite the great wave of building that has been taking place in the last 20 years, most of the early towns have retained most of their old structures that were worth saving for historic or architectural reasons. Louisville, Nashville, and Columbia (South Carolina) have been somewhat less successful in this respect than the others.

Some of the towns, notably Alexandria (Louisiana) and Columbia (South Carolina), like Atlanta, lost many of their older structures as a result of military action during the Civil War.

In the South, to a much greater degree than in the North, older dwellings have been converted to commercial and other non-residential uses, such as funeral parlors, club houses, real estate offices, libraries, office buildings, civic centers, and the like. In the North, the tendency has been to select less historic large buildings for these purposes, but the South seems not to have built so many sizeable downtown residences in the last 60 years or so, with the result that there are not too many newer places available for commercial use.

At least 60 per cent of the towns have one or more "open" houses or museums, almost all of which are interestingly furnished and well worth visiting. A number of these are maintained as memorials to the Confederacy, such as the first White House of the Confederacy in Montgomery.

Natchez leads all southern towns in the number of fine old houses regularly open to the public. Lexington and Frankfort also have several.

In and around these 48 towns are many outstanding mansions, although this book tries to give the rounded flavor of the early towns and does not restrict itself to large and magnificent buildings. In Virginia are such impressive mansions as Belmont, Morven Park, and Oatlands at Leesburg, North Wales at Warrenton, Woodlawn Plantation near Alexandria, Kenmore and Brompton at Fredericksburg, and Monticello at Charlottesville.

In North Carolina, at New Bern, there is Tryon Palace, a reconstruction. Georgia has the Hill House and the Dearing House at Athens, the Old Executive Mansion at Milledgeville, and Overlook at Macon. In Kentucky, there are Ashland, the Hunt-Morgan House, and Waveland at Lexington, Farmington at Louisville, Clay Hill and Aspen Hall at Harrodsburg, and Federal Hill and Wickland at Bardstown.

Tennessee has Fairvue and Foxland Hall at Gallatin, Belmont, Sunnyside, and Melrose at Nashville, and Clifton Place and the Pillow-Bethel House outside Columbia. In Alabama are the Pope-Spraggins and Bibb Houses at Huntsville, the President's Mansion at Tuscaloosa, and the Gillman Mansion at Selma.

In Mississippi and Louisiana, the great plantation houses at Natchez and near New Orleans are too numerous to single out here.

Architecturally the South presents a wide range of style and influences. The grand Georgian and Federal dwellings which are so numerous in the northern states also are prominent in Virginia and Kentucky but are less in evidence further to the south. The Jeffersonian Classical, as it is known locally, comes very much into prominence in Virginia, especially at Monticello, the fine home Jefferson designed for himself.

Greek Revival, with its wide porticos and stunning white columns, is to be seen in Lexington and Harrodsburg, but further down in Georgia, Alabama, and Mississippi and in Louisiana's ante-bellum plantation houses, it seems to all but take over architecturally.

Intermingled are the plainer houses of an earlier era—the raised platform houses such as Gorgas House at Tuscaloosa and many of the earlier plantation homes in Louisiana, the Spanish provincial buildings such as Connelly's Tavern, The Elms, and the Old Spanish House in Natchez, and the creole style in New Orleans' French Quarter with courtyards and ironwork balconies. But to many visitors, the memory of the great Greek Revival mansions will dominate their memories of architecture in this part of the nation, which is not surprising because a large percentage of the houses worthy of mention were not erected until after 1820, when Greek Revival began to attain its wide popularity in this country.

The oldest, and one of the most charming, of the houses pictured in the book may be Roaring Springs, a simple clapboarded farmhouse with exquisite interior woodwork, located just outside Gloucester. Its closest rival is the Cupola House near the water front in Edenton, erected in 1712.

The oldest structure apparently is Ware Church, also near Gloucester, which was constructed soon after 1690. St. Helena's Church in Beaufort was erected in 1724, and the Ursiline Convent in New Orleans' French Quarter was completed in 1734.

Brompton, a large brick house in Fredericksburg, dates from about 1730; Helmley, a low dwelling near Berryville, from about 1740, and Earp's Tavern in Fairfax some time prior to 1742. There are other structures pictured that are known to have been built before the Revolution, but for which no definite date appears to be available.

Of the 370-some buildings pictured, 51 date from before the Revolution, of which 26 are in Virginia and 15 in North Carolina. Another 75 were constructed before the end of 1800, while nearly 80 were built after 1840.

The number of run-down and deteriorating mansions is greater than one might wish in these southern states, but those that were well built by competent artisans in the first place are still in their glory, whether serving as private homes or as museums for public enjoyment. It seems probable, also, that many of those that have not been kept up would have been better maintained had they been built 50 or 100 years earlier, and hence had a stronger and more authentic historic appeal. After all, a large house that is 100 years old usually doesn't compare in value or tradition with one that was built 200 or 250 years ago.

It is obvious, however, that so many of the South's larger and more spectacular homes, as well as some of its smaller but nevertheless historically significant dwellings, have been well enough constructed and are sufficiently well appreciated to guarantee that they will be there for everyone to see and appreciate for many more years to come. Southerners are just as proud of their heritage as the people of the North.

Alexandria, Virginia

ALTHOUGH ITS POPULATION HAS SKY-rocketed past 100,000 by pushing out to the north and west, Old Alexandria on the west bank of the Potomac River just south of Washington, D.C., still retains much of the intimacy and charm it possessed in the mid-1700's when the official surveyor, assisted by young George Washington, laid out a town of 84 half-acre lots in neat squares. It is there that many of the old town houses still stand. As late as 1900, Alexandria still was a community of fewer than 15,000 persons.

Among its claims to fame, Alexandria is noted as the home town and military headquarters of Washington, and Robert E. Lee spent his boyhood there. It was the nearest town of any size for George Mason, author of Virginia's Bill of Rights, and many other notables visited there.

Mount Vernon is only a few miles to the south of Alexandria, and Washington also had a small town house there which he and his family used when they went there for entertainment and other purposes.

Alexandria was first settled in 1670, after Governor Berkeley granted 6,000 acres of land in the vicinity to Robert Howsing, who sold it a later to Captain John Alexander, for whom the town subsequently was named.

Plantations began to grow up soon after 1700, and the new town saw a brisk tobacco trade. Alexandria was a busy seaport in those early days when the largest ocean-going vessels were small enough to sail up the Potomac to its wharfs. Later on, wheat also became an important item of export, but the bulk of the town's ocean trade eventually shifted up to Baltimore, which had become a railroad terminus. Alexandria now has some light industry but is primarily a residential community.

The town was incorporated in 1779, and then in 1789 became part of the new District of Columbia, which kept it until 1846.

A number of sizeable houses were built in early Alexandria, along with many smaller ones, but few approached in size the larger houses in nearby Annapolis, Maryland's capital, or the spacious plantation homes in Virginia's countryside. Many of the early houses are long and narrow with small yards, usually in the rear. The doorways of most houses are flush with the sidewalk, and row houses are not uncommon. Most of the better built early homes have been modernized or restored inside, but the exteriors are little changed.

George Washington recruited and trained in Alexandria his first regiment to fight the French and Indians in 1754 and ended his military career there in 1799.

During the Civil War, the Federal troops seized the town shortly after hostilities broke out, so its buildings escaped the devastation that occurred in other Virginia towns.

Lee House. This is the entrance to the boyhood home of Robert E. Lee. The Federal mansion was built in 1795 by John Potts. It has a central hall with two rooms on each side and a graceful staircase. The dining room is in a wing on a lower level. A spacious garden adjoins the house, replete with shrubs, flowers, and rose beds.

Gadsby's Tavern. This is the cobblestone courtyard of the old tavern, built in 1752 and 1792, where the stagecoaches unloaded their passengers. The spire in the rear is part of the City Hall. George Washington was a frequent visitor to the tavern, as were Lafayette, George Mason, and Franklin. Washington reviewed his troops for the last time from the doorway of the tavern. (Open)

Lower Prince Street. A picturesque row of old colonial and post-colonial homes lines cobblestoned Prince Street, back of a row of Lombardy poplars, as it runs down toward the Potomac River.

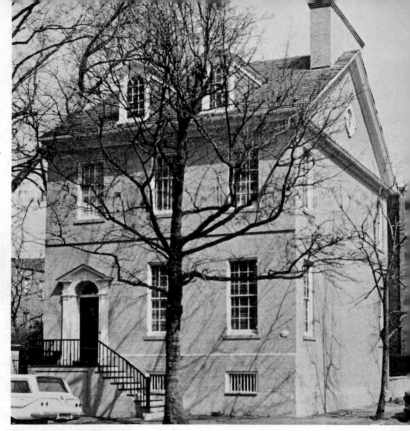

Benjamin Dulany House. The rather plain exterior gives no hint of the magnificent woodwork to be found in the house built in about 1783 by Benjamin Dulany, horseman and aristocrat and intimate of George Washington, whose ward became his wife. Lafayette once made a speech from the small front porch.

Benjamin Dulany House. The narrow entrance hallway leads through a small archway beneath a cornice to the staircase along one side of the house.

Benjamin Dulany House. The imposing
mantel and overmantel are in the drawing
room.

Lafayette House. Thomas Lawrason built this well-designed house in 1795, and his niece lent it to Lafayette, who stayed there on his last visit to America. The attractive interior woodwork is well preserved, and the house is furnished with splendid antiques

115 South Asaph Street. Recognizable by the circular window in the broken pediment over its entrance, the house was built in about 1779. Thomson Mason, brother of George Mason, later made his home there. Old corner fireplaces add charm to the interior, and there is a beautiful low-walled garden.

Dr. Brown House. This pre-Revolutionary house was built by Dr. William Brown, who was a physician-general and director of hospitals of the Continental Army. He had there his personal herb garden needed in connection with his practice. The newer front wing is clapboard over brick. This view shows the older part of the building, which houses the old kitchen.

321 South Asaph Street. This is one of Alexandria's interesting flounder houses which usually lie against an adjoining building with a roof slanting in one direction, possibly because they were expected to become part of a larger structure. It was built in the mid-1700's and contains interesting antiques and old pewter and silver.

Dr. Brown House. The paneled wall with recessed bookcases is at an end of the upstairs library.

Dr. Brown House. An array of copper utensils is seen next to the old kitchen fireplace with its Dutch oven.

Dr. Brown House. The handsome display of pewter and old plates stands along a kitchen wall.

211 Wilkes Street. The narrow town house beneath the two dormers has its front door below grade, indicating that the first floor may once have housed a shop. It was built in the late 1700's. A second-floor drawing room has its original woodwork and old family furniture.

321 South Lee Street. John Davis, a lumber merchant, built the front part of this flounder house in 1830. It has three original mantels and an interesting collection of snuffboxes and pewter.

521 South Lee Street. This town house with its attractive garden in the rear was built about 1794 on land which originally belonged to William Thornton Alexander, son of John Alexander for whom the town was named.

Woodlawn Plantation. A square, rose-red brick house, Woodlawn was designed by William Thornton and finished in 1805. The 2000-acre estate, once part of Mount Vernon, was willed by George Washington to his nephew, Lawrence Lewis, who became the husband of Nellie Custis, granddaughter of Martha Washington. Situated on the crest of a tall but gently rising hill, its front portico looks toward Mount Vernon. There is another entrance facing a large courtyard. The house has two long central halls connected by an elliptical stairway. (Open)

Woodlawn. The harp and other musical instruments are in the music room on the first floor.

Woodlawn. The extensive inside folding shutters help to darken the music room.

Woodlawn. The handsome side-table with its knife and fork boxes stands in the dining room.

Woodlawn. The graceful curved desk is
in a sitting room next to the mantel.

Woodlawn. The doll house with its rock-
ing horse and toys is seen in a hall bedroom.

Woodlawn. The small writing desk and chaise longue appear in the white bedroom.

Woodlawn. This is the graceful winding stairway that connects the two central halls.

Woodlawn. Among the remaining out-buildings is this elaborate smokehouse.

Woodlawn. The "necessary" or outhouse stands just a short distance from the mansion.

Fairfax, Virginia

THE TOWN OF FAIRFAX, SITUATED A SHORT distance west of Washington, D.C., became the county seat of Fairfax County in 1799, when the court was moved from Alexandria, after that part of the state had been ceded to the Federal government as the site of its capital. The town, like the county, was named for Thomas Lord Fairfax.

Some of the old buildings pictured here are a few miles out in the county rather than in the present town, but the entire county may be converted into a municipality to prevent cities within the county from annexing additional lands and thus depleting county revenues.

The town of Fairfax grew around a tavern called Earp's Ordinary, built before 1742. The courthouse, built there after Fairfax became the county seat, was erected on land donated by Richard Ratcliffe of Maryland, who owned a race track in town and also was a merchant and planter. At least, he sold four acres for one dollar to be "used for a courthouse, gaol, and other necessary buildings." He laid out the town in 1805 after the passage of an act by the Assembly.

Two skirmishes occurred there in November, 1861, and by the end of the next year the town came under the command of a Unionist, Brigadier General Edwin H. Stoughton, who later was discharged by President Lincoln.

Among the early buildings in the town was Fairfax Tavern where, on October 1, 1861, Confederate President Jefferson Davis, General Joseph E. Johnson, General P. G. T. Beauregard, and General Gustavus W. Smith held a conference and decided that, in spite of their success at the first Battle of Manassas (Bull Run), the Confederate troops were in no condition to begin an offensive against the city of Washington.

Earp's Tavern. This old hostelry of two or three bedrooms was built before 1742 and is the place around which the town of Fairfax developed.

Antonia Ford House. Built in about 1800, this was the home of a charming Confederate lady who entertained Union officers for the purpose of spying on them. Major James E. Willard, who arrested Miss Ford for giving information to Colonel John S. Mosby and delivered her to prison, later worked for her release and then married her. It now is an office building. (Open)

Fairfax Courthouse. The little red court-house with its arcaded logia and cupola was built in 1800. The wills of George and Martha Washington are displayed in a modern wing of the courthouse. A statue of Captain John Q. Marr, believed to be the first Confederate to die in battle, stands on the courthouse green.

Mosby-Stoughton House. Now the Episcopal rectory, this pre-Civil War dwelling is where Colonel Mosby and 29 men found General Stoughton asleep after stealing through Union picket lines in 1863. It is said they awakened him with a spanking.

Frying Pan Church. The Reverend Jeremiah Moore, who became a Baptist dissenter, was a preacher in this church, built prior to 1772. It is a frame building with wide floor boards, heavy exposed interior timbers, and a circular pulpit.

Sully Plantation. The plantation house was built in about 1794 by Richard Bland Lee, a member of the Virginia House of Delegates, on a grant made by Lord Fairfax in 1725 to Henry Lee, father of the builder. Although one first floor room was added shortly after the house was built, the house never has been restored. It has its original weatherboard and almost all of the original floors, doors, mantels, and trim. (Open)

Sully Plantation. The kitchen and wash house were located in the same detached building near the house. The fireplace has a well-charred wooden lintel.

Sully Plantation. Cracks between the logs in the walls of the kitchen house are filled in with small pieces of rock.

Sully Plantation. The drawing room, once two parlors, now has twin corner fireplaces, back to back. One has been bricked in.

Sully Plantation. The silver wine cups in the antique bookcase were a gift from George Washington.

Sully Plantation. The step-ends of the staircase are hand-carved.

Sully Plantation. A dough box rests next to the sturdy old desk.

Sully Plantation. The large linen chest in a second-floor bedroom has a full-length mirror.

Sully Plantation. In front of the spool bed is an old cradle. On the left is a wash stand with bowl and pitcher.

Sully Plantation. Even the children had a spool bed.

Leesburg, Virginia

THE DATE WHEN LEESBURG WAS FIRST settled is obscured, but it is known that there was a settlement there before 1758, named Georgetown, which was an outfitting post for the French and Indian War in 1755–1759.

In 1758, the Virginia Council authorized the erection of a town there, close to the Potomac River some 45 miles west and north of Washington, D.C. It was named for Francis Lightfoot Lee, a signer of the Declaration of Independence, local land owner, and later a leader in the Revolution.

Ludwell Lee, another Revolutionary officer, built a home nearby and established himself there permanently, but Francis Lightfoot Lee eventually returned to Richmond County in Tidewater Virginia.

Another prominent local resident was President James Madison, who served as a justice in Loudoun County after having served as President of the United States.

What is described as Leesburg's greatest social event occurred in 1825 when Lafayette returned to this country and was entertained at two homes—Belmont and Oak Hill—the latter being the home of then former President Monroe. In appreciation of his fine reception, Lafayette later sent marble mantels which still are treasured at both homes.

One of Leesburg's chief claims to fame occurred right after the British burned Washington in 1814, and wagons bringing government archives reached Leesburg for safekeeping at Rokeby and elsewhere.

Again during the Civil War, Leesburg was a center of activity. Lee's army halted there after its victory at Manassas en route to Sharpsburg, and Confederate General Jubal Early crossed the Potomac nearby after his raid on Washington in 1864. Previously, General Jeb Stuart had camped there on the return from his raid around McClellan's Union army in 1862.

In addition, Mosby's Rangers brought the war to Leesburg in a dramatic way, with frequent raids on convoys and camps in the vicinity, holding down strong detachments of Union troops in the area.

Belmont. Ludwell Lee, son of Richard Henry Lee of the noted Virginia family, built this dark red brick five-part home in 1800. President Madison is said to have spent a brief time there and to have used the house as his headquarters after the burning of the White House, thus making Leesburg the temporary capital of the United States. Later Belmont became a school for young ladies.

Belmont. The hand-carved stairway with interesting step-ends and wainscoting rises from the entrance hall back of a wide arch.

Belmont. This is one of two marble mantels sent back to the mansion by a grateful Lafayette after he made his visit there.

Exeter. Dr. Wilson Cary Selden, who married a niece of George Mason, built Exeter between 1792 and 1800. Though the exterior now is time-worn in appearance, the interior contains delicate woodwork, especially the mantels. The dining room is located in a wing under a domed ceiling. The central portion is built of brick with a clapboard facing.

Oldest Brick House. This pre-Revolutionary house is said to be the oldest brick dwelling in Leesburg.

Thomas E. Cox House. The right-hand portion of this house, with its off-center chimney, was built just after the Revolution. It has its original kitchen with a large fireplace and old utensils.

The Parsonage. The brick portion of this house was built in 1780 as the parsonage for a nearby Methodist church which has disappeared.

Presbyterian Church. The old brick church with its two entrances was erected in 1804. The church bell is under the cupola. (Open)

Morven Park. This plaster-covered stone mansion at the end of a very long lane was built in about 1825 by Thomas Swann, Governor of Maryland. The balcony behind the four massive columns leads to a bedroom.

Dr. Morrison's Office. This old stone house built before the Revolution was used to confine Hessian prisoners of war. (Open)

Dr. Morrison's Office. To amuse themselves, the prisoners drew sketches on the plaster walls of the attic where they were confined.

Dr. Morrison's Office. These are the original roof boards and heavy timbers, fastened with wooden pins.

Rokeby. The L-shaped house is believed to have been built by an Englishman in about 1754. Charles Binns was an early occupant, if not the first. The dining room and drawing room are notable for their carved mantels and arched cabinets built in on either side of the fireplaces.

Rokeby. This medallion appears on the ceiling of the spacious entrance hall. In 1814, when British invasion of Washington was imminent, valuable government documents were carried out to Rokeby for safekeeping. Among them may have been the Declaration of Independence and the Constitution of the United States.

Oatlands. The large porticoed mansion was built about 1799–1802 by George Carter, grandson of Robert "King" Carter. The builder was his own architect and laid out the mansion's splendid terraced gardens and boxwood lanes. The house has become the property of the National Trust for Historic Preservation. (To be open)

Oatlands. The fan-lighted front entrance is ornamented by notable wood carving for which the house is famous.

Oatlands. The arched doorway leads to a stairhall on the first floor at the side of the great entrance hall. There is an identical stairway at each end of the house.

Oatlands. Each of the first floor rooms has a delicate plaster cornice. The drawing room is octagonal in shape.

Berryville, Virginia

GENERAL DANIEL MORGAN, HERO OF THE battle of Cowpens, and Nelly Custis Lewis, granddaughter of Martha Washington, were the most prominent early residents of the Berryville area, originally known as Battletown. Morgan was one of the trustees of the town when it was established 25 miles west of Leesburg in 1798. Mrs. Lewis lived at nearby Audley just prior to her death.

The first residents were Joseph Hampton and two sons who came there from the eastern shore of Maryland in 1774 and lived in a hollow sycamore tree on nearby Buck Marsh, just north of the present downtown area.

The town was established on 20 acres belonging to Benjamin Berry and Sarak Stribling, but later was enlarged by the purchase of additional land from Charles Smith. The latter land was part of a grant made by the Crown in 1734 to Isaac Pendleton.

The Shawnee tribe lived nearby but there is no record of raids or massacres.

The young town quickly acquired a blacksmith shop, a wagonmaking establishment, and a general store, plus a tavern. Plows also were made there. A stone school, known as Berryville Academy, was built in about 1810.

Nothing of great moment appears to have happened at any time, although in the Civil War, Generals Early and Sheridan fought the Battle of Berryville in September, 1864, and Colonel Mosby engaged the Sixth New York Cavalry at Buck Marsh a few days later.

Morgan Spring. Bushrod Taylor built the large house in about 1825. The tower for the music room was added later. The interior woodwork and fireplace tiles are especially interesting.

Morgan Spring. The meat house standing near the mansion is uniquely glorified by the Ionic columns and the flight of steps in front of its entrance.

Audley. Warner Washington, a cousin of George Washington, built Audley in 1774 on land conveyed by Lord Fairfax. The house later was owned by Lawrence Lewis, son of George Washington's sister, Betty Lewis, and is where Nelly Custis Lewis lived in her later years.

Fairfield. The handsome gray stone mansion was built in 1770 by the same Warner Washington who later built Audley. It has a fine terraced garden with circles of old boxwood.

Helmley. The simple English cottage built prior to 1734 by Meredith Helm may be the oldest house in northwestern Virginia. Of stone and frame construction, it is furnished with fine antiques.

Milton Valley. The two-part stone house was built in 1782 by John Milton and still has its old stone barn and smoke house. Its numerous antiques include a rare collection of spurs and stirrups from all over the world.

Milton Valley. The fireplace end of the living room is paneled, as are the window recesses.

Milton Valley. The chest in front of the wainscoting and the portrait are seen in the front hall.

Milton Valley. The table and silver service under the Japanese painting are located in the dining room under a delicate cornice.

Woodley. The spacious brick house wi[th] a superb view of the mountains was bu[ilt] in about 1834 by Daniel Sowers. It h[as] beautiful cherry doors made from trees c[ut] on the premises and rare old Chinese lot[us] china.

Woodley. The interesting stairway rises from the side of the wide hall that runs from front to back.

Woodley. The dining room is furnished with excellent antiques and old silver.

Woodley. More antiques are seen in the drawing room in front of a splendid mantel.

Woodley. This fine old furniture appears in the cheerful parlor.

Annefield. Another large gray stone building, Annefield was erected in 1790 by Matthew Page and named after his wife, a sister of Episcopal Bishop William Meade. The interior woodwork shows excellent craftsmanship and is well-proportioned.

Old Chapel. The little ivy-covered stone building was erected in 1790. Bishop Meade, known as the church historian, preached there for many years.

Springsbury. John Holker, a first consul from France, built the central part of the house in 1792. The dining-room wallpaper was made by DuFour in Paris in 1810. Bow-paned windows contain collections of old glass.

Warrenton, Virginia

SETTLERS WENT TO WARRENTON AS EARLY as 1712, and Thomas Lee, a descendant of Richard Lee, the original family settler from England, received a grant of 4200 acres in the vicinity in 1718. The town was named for General William Warren, a hero of Bunker Hill.

Situated 45 miles south and west of Washington, D.C., it was surveyed and laid out in 1791 by James Routte under the direction of Thomas Lee's son, Richard Henry Lee. At that time it was called Fauquier Courthouse.

Charles Lee, a naval officer during the Revolution and U.S. Attorney General under George Washington, lived close by in a house known as Leeton Forest. John Marshall, U.S. Chief Justice, was born just nine miles away.

When Lafayette went there in 1825, he was met by Captain Walder's light infantry, Captain Shocklett's cavalry, the Marine Band from Washington, and a group of 50 to 60 "well dressed young boys" who formed Lafayette's guard. A sumptuous dinner was served under a spacious arbor on the green in front of a tavern, with Colonel William R. Randolph presiding. Nearly 20 toasts were drunk.

Captain Marr, believed to be the first Confederate to fall in battle, was a native of Warrenton.

In 1863, Warrenton was the scene of a fight between troops led by Colonel John S. Mosby and a Union detachment which he surprised and captured. Later he was overtaken by other Union forces and barely escaped after losing his prisoners. Troops which fought at nearby Manassas were quartered at Warrenton.

After the war, Mosby moved to Warrenton, where he was arrested by the Federal government. After his release, he practiced law there.

Today the town is the social capital of Virginia's "horsey" folk.

Fauquier Club. This modest town residence built in about 1840 contains beautiful woodwork brought from England, where it was carved by Grinling Gibbons. Today the building is a private club house.

Old Norris House. The charming brick house, with its side to the street, was built about 1800 by Thaddeus Norris, a prosperous inn and hotel owner. The newel post and bannister are made of fruitwood, and the house has its original mantels, woodwork, and heart pine floors.

Clovelly. Formerly known as Cedar Grove, the oldest part of the farmhouse was built in about 1746 by Peter Kemper. It stands on a small hill and enjoys a sweeping view of the rolling countryside to the south.

Clovelly. The parlor fireplace has a handsomely carved mantel.

Clovelly. Another example of fine wood-work is the interior doorway, standing beneath the exposed ceiling beams.

North Wales. The first part of the large stone mansion, which later was owned by Walter Chrysler, Jr., was erected in about 1773 by William Allison of Glasgow, Scotland. Its foundations are six feet thick. The interior features are the hand-carved paneling and other woodwork.

Woodbourne. The T-shaped stone house was built prior to 1800. It was the home of Isaac Keith, a soldier of the Revolution, whose sister was the mother of Chief Justice Marshall.

Woodbourne. The old well, operated by a crank, is one of the interesting attractions of the large garden.

Fauquier Springs. This building is about all that remains of a once large resort, known before the Civil War as one of the most fashionable watering spots in the East. It had a huge ballroom and accomodations for 600 guests. This structure was part of the bachelors' quarters.

Oakwood. Judge John Scott built the house in about 1805. It is admired for its graceful stairway, paneled doors with old brass locks, and well-proportioned rooms.

Charlottesville, Virginia

PETER JEFFERSON ACQUIRED THE ESTATES known as Shadwell and Monticello and, according to his son, Thomas Jefferson, was the third or fourth settler in the region when he went there in about 1737. The earliest land patents were dated 1727, but very few early patentees settled their estates.

The county purchased 1000 acres from Richard Randolph, laid out 50 acres in streets and lots near the Rivanna River 65 miles northwest of Richmond, and built a courthouse in 1761. The town established by the General Assembly was named for Queen Charlotte, wife of George III. Stores and taverns sprang up quickly and, until well into the 1800's, the chief avenue of commerce was the river.

The Revolution did not prove too upsetting for Charlottesville, although there was activity on two occasions. The first was in 1779 when prisoners taken after Burgoyne's surrender at Saratoga were transferred down there and held; the second occasion was when British Colonel Banastre Tarleton conducted a raid in 1781 and destroyed military stores and ransacked the courthouse.

In the Civil War, Union forces under General William T. Sheridan occupied the town in the last year of the war, but did little damage.

Besides being the home of Thomas Jefferson, James Monroe lived in Charlottesville, and both George Rogers Clark and Meriwether Lewis, noted pioneers and explorers, were born nearby. The University of Virginia was founded there by Jefferson in 1819.

Courthouse. The red brick courthouse of Albemarle County was partly built in 1803 and then enlarged in 1860. The tall portico in Ionic style was added in the 1870's. The north wing was used as a church in its early days. The archives contain some of Thomas Jefferson's correspondence. (Open)

The Rotunda. Begun in 1822 to serve as the university's library, the rotunda closes the north end of the lawn. It is an adaptation of one-half the diameter of the Pantheon in Rome. (Open)

The Rotunda. Two-story columns support the top structure of the rotunda on the interior.

The Lawn. The large open lawn, or green, is terraced and bordered with trees. Five two-story pavillions in a variety of classical styles line each side. Their construction began in 1817.

Serpentine Walls. The low red brick walls, which average about six feet in height, surround the gardens near the lawn. They are just one brick thick and were laid in the serpentine design to add strength. Jefferson designed them, based on a practice he had observed in France.

Monroe House. On the crest of Monroe Hill is a brick house, painted white, that James Monroe purchased or built when he first went to the county in 1790. He lived there until he moved to nearby Ash Lawn. He had his law office in an arcaded outbuilding.

Michie Tavern. The old part of the hostelry was built before 1740 and has fine interior woodwork. It was enlarged in 1763 after Major John Henry, father of Patrick Henry, sold it to John Michie. It contains colonial tavern furnishings. (Open)

Monticello. This home of Thomas Jefferson is located on a beautiful wooded estate, now containing 650 acres, on the leveled top of a small mountain with a marvellous view of the crest of the Blue Ridge Mountains and the Piedmont across its wide lawn. The red brick mansion with snow white trim, which Jefferson designed, was started in 1770. It has excellent interior woodwork. A large entrance hall opens beneath a balcony into the salon. Lateral halls lead to four chambers, the dining room, and Jefferson's study. Two steep staircases to the second floor are hidden in closet-like alcoves. At his death in 1826, the estate was valued at $70,000 but, in depressed times in 1831, the house and 552 acres sold for one-tenth that amount. (Open)

Monticello. This old kitchen, used by the slaves, is located beneath a terrace close to the mansion.

Monticello. The elaborate domed well-house is seen a short distance from the mansion.

Ash Lawn. James Monroe built this unretentious house in 1796–1798 in order to be near Jefferson. He had planned a much larger place but never completed it. Then, in 1820, he moved to Oak Hill, a beautiful mansion south of Leesburg. (Open)

Morven. This brick house is located on part of a 10,000-acre grant made to one of the sons of Robert "King" Carter. David Higginbotham built the house in about 1820. It contains two marble mantels selected by Thomas Jefferson.

Fredericksburg, Virginia

ALTHOUGH IT PROVIDED BOTH ARMY AND arms for the Continental forces during the Revolution, Fredericksburg escaped bloodshed. But lying on a main road and rail line between Washington and Richmond, it was far less fortunate during the Civil War when it changed hands seven times and became one of the bloodiest battlefields in history.

George Washington's mother spent her last years there, and it was the home of Betty Lewis, George's sister. Fredericksburg also was where James Monroe practiced law before gaining the Presidency.

Fredericksburg, lying on the Rappahannock River, was visited by Captain John Smith in 1608. A tract was patented there in 1671, and in 1727 the General Assembly directed that 30 acres be set aside and laid out for a town to be named after Frederick, Prince of Wales and father of King George III. It was incorporated in 1781.

At the head of navigation on the river, the town became the center for a large and fertile agricultural region and grew steadily as a port for shipping tobacco, wheat, butter, cheese, flax, and hemp. Products of the local plantations came to town in large canvas-covered wagons, some of them 12 feet high and drawn by four to eight horses. Often there were as many as 200 of the huge wagons in town at one time, bringing cargoes for many vessels, some of them three-masted schooners.

The town was half burned in 1807 but recovered to become a social and commercial center for many slave-holding, landed proprietors and entered a period when "racecourses, wine cellars, and balls reached their apogee."

Mary Washington House. This is the garden side of the house built in 1772 by George Washington for his mother. Her sun dial and boxwood are still there in an old-fashioned garden with a path that once led up to Kenmore, her daughter's grand home. George Washington was a frequent visitor to his mother's home. Other prominent guests included Thomas Jefferson, George Mason, Lafayette, and members of the Lee family. (Open)

Mary Washington House. The four-poster with the bed steps rests in a first-floor bedroom.

Mary Washington House. In the far corner of the dining room, is a chaise in which the President's mother rode back and forth to Ferry Farm across the Rappahannock River.

Kenmore. Fielding Lewis, husband of George Washington's sister Betty, started this magnificent mansion in 1752 on land surveyed by Washington, who was a frequent visitor there. It served as a hospital and military headquarters during the Civil War and later became a boys' school. Much of the exquisite furniture and many of the relics seen in the house were the property of the Washington and Lewis families. The woodwork, ceilings, and much of the hardware and flooring are original, although the two detached flanking dependencies are reconstructed. (Open)

Kenmore. The elaborate mantel and overmantel are in the great room under a handsome cornice.

Kenmore. The first floor ceilings are embellished with rich plaster ornamentation.

Kenmore. This beautiful secretary is typical of the fine furnishings to be seen throughout the mansion.

Kenmore. Even the children's room had a small four-poster.

Kenmore. It is said that George Washington, exhausted from a long trip, once threw himself on this bed without taking time to remove his clothing.

Kenmore. This is a corner of a lady's bedroom, showing one of several recessed window seats.

Kenmore. One of the detached dependencies contains an old kitchen fireplace and furnishings with herbs drying in front of the wooden lintel. On the wall of the kitchen is this array of old-time utensils.

John Paul Jones House. This pre-Revolutionary house, half brick and half frame, is the only place in the United States where John Paul Jones, the naval hero, resided for any extended period. He went there in about 1768 after seven years at sea. It was the home of his brother, William Paul, a tailor, who had migrated there from Scotland.

Federal Hill. The white clapboard siding covers walls of brick in the pre-Revolutionary house, once owned by Governor Robert Brooke. A paneled transverse hall, with a splendid staircase, leads through an elegant arched doorway into a drawing room that runs the full length of the house.

Brompton. The center of this mellow old house, which shows scars of Civil War battles, was built in about 1730 by Colonel Henry Willis. For a time it served as the headquarters of General Robert E. Lee. The house and garden have been restored, and this is now the home of the Chancellor of Mary Washington College.

Brompton. The mantel and fireplace are
at the end of the drawing room.

Brompton. This wide hallway leads
through the arch into the splendidly furnished drawing room.

Gloucester, Virginia

ANY HISTORY OF GLOUCESTER, FORMERLY known as Botetourt Town and as Gloucester Court House, is necessarily brief because early town and parish records were lost when the County Clerk's office burned in 1820, and because records for the period from 1820 to 1860 also were lost after they were taken to Richmond for safekeeping during the Civil War, being burned when the Confederate Capital, 70 miles to the northwest, was evacuated.

It is known that in 1769 the Governor approved an act of the General Assembly authorizing John Fox, "gentleman," to lay off 60 acres of his land, adjoining the lands on which the courthouse of the County of Gloucester is erected, into lots and streets for a town to be called and known as Botetourt Town, in honor of Norborne Berkley Botetourt, then governor of the colony.

On the walls of the courthouse hang portraits of Gloucester's famous sons, including Lieutenant Philip Tabb of Revolutionary days.

Roaring Springs. This small manor house, probably the oldest pictured in this book, was built about 1700. An early owner was Francis Thornton, who sold it to James Baytop Taliaferro. It contains furnishings that once belonged to Johns Hopkins, an ancestor of the present owner. A series of pools in the large yard are fed by enormous springs, from which the house takes its name.

Roaring Springs. The drawing room is superbly paneled, with arched recesses on either side of the fireplace.

Roaring Springs. The parlor is one of the show rooms of the manor house.

Walter Reed's Birthplace. Built in the early 1800's, this little three-room house was the birthplace of Walter Reed, the discoverer of the cause of yellow fever. His father was a clergyman whose home burned down just three weeks before Reed was born, forcing the family to move into the tiny quarters.

County Courthouse. The small brick courthouse was erected in 1766. It contains 48 portraits of famous sons and seven tablets, including one which characterizes Nathaniel Bacon, leader of the Virginia rebellion of 1676, as a "soldier, statesman, and saint." (Open)

Long Bridge Ordinary. This was a well-known hostelry in colonial days and until the Civil War. It was erected on a hillside in about 1727. The lower story, which is the basement, is made of brick and the upper stories are of frame construction. It has five fireplaces but only one chimney. It now is the home of the Gloucester Woman's Club. (Open)

Ware Church. This sturdily built church, erected soon after 1690 and surrounded by a low brick wall, has foundations that are six feet deep and five feet wide, but are only as high as the ground level. The walls are three feet thick, and the rafters measure 12 by 18 inches. Its communion service was presented to a nearby church by Augustine Warner in 1681. (Open)

Ware Church. A long paneled wall extends across the back of the church under the balcony.

Goshen. Situated at the head of the Ware River, Goshen was built about 1750 or later. Originally it consisted of two grand wainscoted rooms separated by a central hall. The wings and another addition were built later. A slave cabin and smokehouse remain near the house.

Goshen. Handsome woodwork adds interest to the drawing room with its arched openings.

Loretta. Except for the addition of wing, this house orginally built in abo 1783 and since restored, is today as it w when it was the home of General Willia R. Davis, delegate to the Constitutio Convention, governor of the state, a Minister Plenipotentiary to France.

Halifax, North Carolina

IN THE EARLY DAYS, HALIFAX IS SAID TO have been known for its grace, gaiety, and opulence, and its early society has been characterized as the most cultured and polished in the state.

In those times, the little town was quite active politically, having been the scene of North Carolina's first Constitutional Convention. Moreover, the Provincial Congress met there in 1776 in the early courthouse, and the presiding officer appointed a committee to "take into account the usurpations and violences attempted and committed by the King and Parliament of Britain against America."

The committee reported, designating a delegation to attend the Continental Congress ". . . to concur with delegates from other colonies in declaring independency and forming foreign alliances."

These Halifax Resolves, as they were called, are said to constitute the first action by any colonial legislature for absolute separation from Great Britain and for national independence.

A wedding in Halifax in 1790 was celebrated in 22 consecutive dinner parties in as many houses and terminated in a great ball. But by the following year, as noted by George Washington, the town's social reputation already had begun to wane.

Halifax, located a few miles south of the Virginia line in the eastern part of the state, was settled in 1723 and named for the second Earl of Halifax, president of the British Board of Trade. It was laid out in 1758 with a courthouse green of four acres and became the county seat in that year.

Old Confederate Hospital. The small, pre-Revolutionary frame house which had interesting interior paneling and mantels has been described as a perfect example of Dutch colonial architecture. It, too, has been restored.

Masonic Temple. This is the home of a lodge originated in 1769 and is one of the oldest built for that special purpose. The first floor was used as a school until 1829.

Clerk's Office. The small brick building, which originally housed the county clerk, later became a printing office and then a library. Built in about 1780, it has stone lintels over its openings and formerly had swinging iron shutters.

Old Gaol. The construction of this building was authorized by the colonial assembly in 1764. Its brick walls are two feet thick. In 1776 it was used to confine 41 Highland Scotsmen after their defeat in a local engagement.

Eagle Hotel. This pre-Revolutionary hostelry was the headquarters for most of the Provincial Congresses and Assemblies. Among its guests were George Washington, Cornwallis, and Lafayette. In 1845, part of the structure was acquired as a residence and moved to its present site by Michael Ferrall. The double entrance doors have hand-blown glass panels framed by facings ornamented with sunbursts.

St. Mark's Church. Made of wood painted dark gray, the little church was built in 1854. It has vertical siding with overlapping joints and is four bays long.

Constitution House. The Provincial Constitution of 1776 approved by the committee appointed by the Provincial Congress was drafted in this small colonial home. It has been restored and moved from its former site near the colonial cemetery.

Raleigh, North Carolina

JOEL LANE AND HIS BROTHERS, JAMES AND Jesse, arrived in Raleigh and built a house several years before a courthouse and jail were erected in front of their house in 1771, the year when Wake County was formed. Joel Lane built a tavern to accommodate visitors and also helped to build a log church.

The settlement, in the east-central part of the state, was first known as Wake Courthouse, named for Mary Wake, wife of William Tryon, the Royal Governor.

The seat of the state government was located there on a tract of 1000 acres purchased from Lane for £1378, and a town was laid out in 1792 by William Christmas. By 1800, the population had risen to 669 persons, and Methodist Bishop Francis Asbury held a big meeting in the statehouse, which then was used for meetings, balls, religious gatherings, and other important occasions.

The Raleigh Academy for boys and girls opened in 1801, and Casso's Inn, built before 1800, already had become a popular gathering place.

In the Civil War, the city became a concentration point for Confederate troops, and gunpowder and other supplies were manufactured there. General William T. Sherman's army entered without resistance in April, 1865, and promptly received the keys to the capital.

Mordecai House. Joel Lane gave this frame house to his son, Henry, in 1788. It is built of handhewn timbers with wooden pegs. The front of the house, including the two-story portico, was added in 1824 by Moses Mordecai. Lafayette stopped there in 1825.

Richard B. Haywood House. During the Union occupation at the end of the Civil War, this brick house built in 1854 was the headquarters of Union Major Francis P. Blair, Jr., and was visited by Generals Sherman and Grant.

Christ Church. The red-gray stone church was erected between 1848 and 1853. It was designed by Richard Upjohn, the architect of Trinity Church in New York City, based on a medieval parish church in England. Its slender octagonal spire rises to a height of about 100 feet. It was built with slave labor. (Open)

The Old Rectory. Originally constructed as a bank in about 1818, the brick building has granite lintels and double-gallery porticos in both front and back.

The Capitol. The carved ornamental detail in the halls and public rooms employs both Ionic and Corinthian forms.

The Capitol. The cornerstone was laid in 1833 and the structure was completed in 1840 under the supervision of David Paton, who imported stone masons from Scotland for the job. It is built of granite quarried nearby. (Open)

The Capitol. Elaborate arches stretch overhead.

The Capitol. This is the handsome entrance to a legislative chamber.

The Capitol. The interior of the rotunda has a height of 93½ feet.

Dr. Johnson House. Although the portico was added much later, the frame house was started before the Civil War. It was the home of Dr. Charles E. Johnson, North Carolina's Surgeon General during the war, and now is church property. A balcony is suspended over the front entrance.

Lane House. Built for Joel Lane prior to 1771, this is the oldest dwelling in the city. It has been restored and moved about 150 feet from its original site and now is the headquarters of the Wake County Committee of the Colonial Dames of America.

Andrew Johnson House. This humble frame dwelling, built prior to 1808, was the birthplace of President Andrew Johnson. It has been moved to a public park and contains Johnson mementos. (Open)

Chapel Hill, North Carolina

THE UNIVERSITY OF NORTH CAROLINA AT Chapel Hill, a few miles northwest of Raleigh, was the first state university to open its doors, which it did in January, 1795, although the first student, who walked part of the way from Wilmington down on the coast, didn't arrive until the middle of February and constituted the entire student body for two weeks.

Either feather beds were rented for $24 a year, or the boys slept on hard boards. Meals at the commons were $40 per year. Some students brought servants with them to forage for wood, carry water, and cook meals.

The site of the town was selected in 1792 under a charter issued by the General Assembly in 1789. The first town lots were sold in 1793. The name of the new town was taken from a little New Hope Chapel of the Established Church of England that stood in the eighteenth century on the road from New Bern to Salisbury.

General William Lenoir was the first president of the Board of Trustees, the other members also being prominent men of the state.

Widow Puckett House. This frame dwelling was built in 1799 for John Puckett and is one of the few remaining examples of early Chapel Hill architecture.

Person Hall. This was the university's first chapel, a gift from General Thomas Person. It was started in 1793 and finished four years later. The H-shaped structure was built in three parts. (Open)

Old East. Believed to be the country's oldest standing state university building, the cornerstone of Old East was laid in 1793. It was designed and built by James Patterson, a mechanic, to serve as a dormitory. It was constructed of brick with mortar made from ground-up sea shells. (Open)

South Building. Although the cornerstone was laid in 1798, a lottery had to be held in 1814 to raise funds with which to complete it. Modeled after Princeton University's Nassau Hall, it now houses administrative offices of the university. (Open)

Old West. This long, ivy-covered dormitory was built in 1824 to match Old East. (Open)

Gerrard Hall. Built in 1822, the building succeeded Person Hall as the university's chapel. (Open)

Governor Ellis House. Archibald Henderson, lawyer and U.S. Congresman, was the first owner of the house built in 1822. He sold it to Mrs. Giles Pearson, sister of Governor John W. Ellis, who lived there prior to his death.

Salisbury, North Carolina

Long before the first courthouse was erected there in 1775, Salisbury had been a campsite for traders and an outpost for land-hungry immigrants—Scotch-Irish and German—taking up lands offered by the Earl of Granville.

As early as 1765, Governor Tryon reported that more than 1000 wagons passed through the town in a single year.

It was from Salisbury, situated northeast of Charlotte, that Daniel Boone was sent by Richard Henderson and Company to blaze a trail into the lands beyond the mountains in what is the present state of Kentucky.

Cornwallis marched through the town, staying only briefly and doing no important damage, in February, 1781, and George Washington came in 1791. The steps from which he spoke to the citizenry in front of a demolished tavern have been preserved.

During the Civil War, the Confederates maintained a prison in Salisbury for Union prisoners, 12,000 of whom died there. When Union General George Stoneman captured the town in April, 1865, he used the same prison for Confederate prisoners after freeing the Union troops being held there.

The present courthouse has records dating back to 1753, including names of important persons, such as Daniel Boone, Andrew Jackson, and General Francis Locke. Andrew Jackson was admitted to the bar in Salisbury in 1787.

Blackmer House. John Foster, a wealthy merchant and civic leader, built this house in 1822 to serve as a girls' school. Later it became the residence of Sidney Blackmer, the actor. Its tall portico is almost obscured by trees.

Chambers House (Rowan Museum). This frame house was built in about 1819 for Judge James Martin, who sold it to the Reverend Thomas F. Davis, rector of St. Luke's Church. Later it was purchased by Maxwell Chambers II and given to the Presbyterian Church, which it served as a manse for over 50 years. It now is a museum. (Open)

Chambers House. An old French clock
and Holland Delft urns stand on the hand-
carved mantel in the parlor.

Chambers House. The handsome pedimented secretary rests in the parlor under
an ornamental plaster cornice.

Chambers House. This lovely Sheraton bed has a straw tick, feather bed and bolster, a dust ruffle, and tester swags.

McNeely-Strachan House. When it was built in 1815, this house was the main building of the Salisbury Academy. It has 12-foot ceilings on the first floor and 14-foot ceilings on the second floor. The ironwork and galleries were added in 1859 by Dr. Joseph W. Hall, and the third floor was added much later.

Law Office. This one-time law office of
Archibald Henderson is believed to be the
oldest unaltered building in Salisbury.

St. Luke's Church. The parish was established in 1753, and the edifice was erected
in 1828 on land donated by John Lewis
Beard. It contains a chalice, paten, and
flagon made from "brooches, rings, chains,
and gifts from loved ones" given at the sug-
gestion of Mrs. Jefferson Davis by the
ladies of St. Lazarus Church in Memphis
for their own church, then given to St.
Luke's when their parish was blotted out.
The gift was made in the memory of the
Reverend John Thomas Wheat, who died
in Salisbury. (Open)

The Old Courthouse. Now a civic center, the old courthouse built in 1854–1857 has a Doric entablature and six Doric columns. (Open)

Beard Building. Erected in 1850, the brick building first was the home of Horace Beard, then became a tailor shop. It now contains offices. (Open)

Edenton, North Carolina

TEMPORARY SETTLERS FIRST CAME TO Edenton, located off Albemarle Sound on Queen Anne Creek, in 1658, and in 1712 the General Assembly passed an act to build a courthouse and a house for the Assembly and appointed a commission to lay out a town there.

The first lot was sold in 1714 to Edward Mosely, who then built the first house in the town. At first it was called "Ye Towne on Queen Anne Creek," but later took the name of Edenton in honor of Governor Charles Eden when it was incorporated in 1722.

The governor lived nearby, and the town served as an unofficial capital for about 40 years.

Edenton was an early seaport, and ship building was an important activity. Local merchants exported pitch, tar, turpentine, tobacco, salt meat, and dried fish. One of the early ship-builders was James Hewes, who also was a signer of the Declaration of Independence. Other prominent citizens included Samuel Johnston, Continental Congressman, governor, and first U.S. Senator from North Carolina, and James Iredell, associate member of the first U.S. Supreme Court. The early homes of all three are still standing and in active use.

During the Revolution, Edenton escaped attack. There was a disturbing report that Cornwallis' troops were on the way at one time, but after many residents panicked and fled the report proved false.

The town's early houses are modest in size, for the most part, but some imposing residences were built during the first half of the nineteenth century.

Blair House. Built about 1755, the frame house originally was occupied by the Blair family and later was the home of Thomas C. Manning, Brigadier General in the Confederate Army, Chief Justice of the Supreme Court of Louisiana, and Ambassador to Mexico.

Iredell House. The galleried house was built prior to 1769 and shortly afterwards became the home of James Iredell, Attorney General of North Carolina and a U.S. Supreme Court Justice by appointment of George Washington. The house later became a rectory for St. Paul's church.

Charlton House. The house was erected in about 1765 for Jaspar Charlton and his wife, Abagail, the first signer of the Tea Party Resolutions.

Hatch House. Also known as O'Malley's Ordinary, this house is believed to have been built about 1744 by Andre Richard, a French barber, for his daughter Lucy and her husband, Edmund Hatch. It became an inn after 1814.

Chowan County Courthouse. Built in 1767, perhaps by Gilbert Leigh, and described as a fine example of Georgian Architecture, the courthouse has been in continuous use ever since. It faces the bay across Edenton Green. (Open)

Chowan County Courthouse. The walls of the second-floor courtroom are elaborately paneled under a handsome cornice and decorated with fine drapes and old portraits of local notables.

Ellison House. Benjamin Ellison, a Tory, owned the house before it was confiscated in 1776. The house was built by Robert Lemar and later became the home of Governor James Iredell, Jr. It was erected prior to 1769.

Ellison House. A sturdy drop-leaf dining table stands in front of a handsome sideboard in the dining room.

Ellison House. Another attractive drop-leaf table rests against a paneled wall under a family portrait in the parlor.

Tea Party Marker. A large bronze teapot marks the site of the Edenton Tea Party. Here in 1774, 51 Edenton ladies, led by Penelope Barker, signed resolutions against the tax on tea, calling it British injustice to the colonies. This is said to be the earliest known instance of political activity by women in the colonies.

Old Cannon. These cannons, dating from Revolutionary days, stand overlooking the bay on the green in front of the courthouse. They were brought from England in 1778. In the background is Barker House, built in about 1782. This was the home of Thomas and Penelope Barker. Barker was a London agent for the colony; his wife was the leader in the Tea Party Resolutions.

Cupola House. Described as an outstanding example of Jacobean architecture, the frame Cupola House was built in about 1712. The octagonal cupola or "lantern" was used for sighting ships at sea. The first floor paneling was sold to the Brooklyn Museum. The house now is a museum. (Open)

New Bern, North Carolina

ALTHOUGH SOME FRENCH HUGUENOTS settled there temporarily in 1707, the first permanent settlement in New Bern was established in 1710 by a group of Palatines and Swiss led by Baron Christopher de Graffenried. The town is named after Berne, Switzerland.

Anxious to help the numerous Palatines who had left Germany and migrated to England, Queen Anne agreed to sponsor some 92 families comprising 600 people to settle in the New World under De Graffenried.

In collaboration with Franz Ludwig Michel, a Swiss whom he had met in Switzerland, De Graffenried formed a group of 650 Palatines selected from all trades and arranged for needed supplies. The group sailed from England under the command of John Lawson, an explorer and writer who owned property in the New Bern area. The trip took 13 weeks, and more than half the party died en route. De Graffenried and Michel sailed from England later with another hundred people.

Soon after the colonists started building homes and grist mills and developing businesses, a plague of yellow fever exacted a heavy toll. Then in 1711 the Tuscarora Indians attacked the settlement, killed more than 150 men, and carried away many women and children as hostages. Both De Graffenried and Lawson were among those captured, but the former claimed he was king of the white men. Since the Indians believed that bad fortune would befall anyone who killed a king, De Graffenried was released and ordered back to England.

The date of the attack was declared a Day of Humiliation by the General Assembly, and for many years it was observed as a day of fasting and prayer.

New Bern, located on the Neuse River some miles west of Pamlico Sound, was incorporated in 1723 and became an important seaport, trading with New England and the rest of the world in the early years. It also was a major supply base during the Civil War, when it was a fortified port of the Confederacy until captured by General Ambrose E. Burnside in 1862.

Historic Cannon. Dating from the Revolution, this old cannon "guards" the town against invasion from the Neuse River.

Blackwell-Bray House. Josiah Blackwell built the little frame section on the right in 1774, and it later became the birthplace of Hannis Taylor, Minister to Spain and authority on international law.

Leech-Guion House. When Joseph Leech built this house in 1803, it consisted of only one room and a hall. The entrance, with the fan-lighted door, is its dominating feature. It was a Federal headquarters during the Civil War.

Stanly House. Now a public library, the handsome house was erected in about 1780-1790 by John Stanly, a merchant, and it was the home of his son, who was a member of Congress. George Washington was a guest there in 1791, and it was General Burnside's headquarters during the Civil War. Later it became a convent. (Open)

Stanly House. The pedimented doorway leads to the front hallway from the parlor.

Attmore-Oliver House. Now the interestingly furnished headquarters of the New Bern Historical Society, the house was built about 1790 by Samuel Chapman, a member of the organization that welcomed George Washington to New Bern in 1791. It has a fireplace in every room and original flooring of wide heart pine. The house contains many photographs of the early days of the city and an extensive file of historic papers. Twin galleries run across the back of the house. (Open)

Attmore-Oliver House. The small brick building back of the house was a combination outside kitchen and meat house.

Attmore-Oliver House. Early furniture graces the dining room, surrounded by old wallpaper.

Attmore-Oliver House. The old desk and chairs are placed in an upstairs bedroom.

Attmore-Oliver House. This furniture, including the early bathtub, miniature bed, and drying rack, is in another bedroom.

Tryon Palace. The palace became the first fixed colonial capitol of North Carolina and also served as the governor's residence in 1770. Construction was started in 1767 under the supervision of John Hawks, an English architect, said to be the first professional architect to remain in America. George Washington was a guest at a banquet there in 1791. The main building was destroyed by fire in 1798 and the east wing did not long survive it. Restoration was begun in 1952 with eighteenth-century material and hardware brought from England and with brick and other material found on the site. The furnishings are genuine eighteenth-century antiques, and the landscaped grounds are designed in the manner of the mid-1700's. The Tryon Palace Commission, a state agency, administers the beautifully restored and furnished building.

Tryon Palace. The large bed is in the governor's bedroom, which like other rooms has richly carved woodwork.

Tryon Palace. The Council Chamber with its paneling and bold cornice is a highlight of the first floor.

Tryon Palace. Several splendidly carved
mantels are seen in the palace.

Beaufort, South Carolina

SEVEN FLAGS HAVE FLOWN OVER BEAU-fort since the Spanish touched there in 1520. After the Spanish came the French flag in 1562, the flag of Scotland in 1613, the English flag in 1663, the flag of the United States in 1776, the flag of the Independent Republic of South Carolina in 1860, and the Confederate flag in 1861. Some flags flew there more than once.

Beaufort prefers to date its beginning from the brief settlement established in the area in 1562 by the Huguenot Jean Rabaut, but it was not until about 1712 that the town of Beaufort was founded by an Englishman, Henry Somerset, Duke of Beaufort.

At first there was only a blockhouse and a few simple dwellings in which generous use was made of tabby, a mixture of oyster shells, lime, sand, and water.

In its early days, Beaufort had its full share of catastrophe. First, the Yamasses Indians massacred many of the settlers in 1715, although several hundred others were able to take refuge on a British ship. Then pirates, yellow fever, smallpox, and hurricanes came to harass the early residents.

The cultivation and export of indigo were responsible for the development of a plantation system in the early days, although the owners built their homes in Beaufort for summer use where the climate was better than in the marshlands.

During the Revolution, the small defenseless town fell quickly to the British. After the war, rice and sea island cotton replaced indigo as temporary sources of new and greater wealth, and larger homes were built.

During the Civil War, Beaufort was occupied for four years by Federal troops, the residents having moved out to the countryside, and thus the town was spared by Sherman's army in its northward march. It remained in the hands of the Federal government during the reconstruction period after the war, when its old homes and plantations were confiscated and sold for taxes. However, the town slowly succeeded in regaining its former charm, which it retains today, "with its shaded streets and old-fashioned gardens where camellias, jessamine, oleander, and wisteria mingle under moss-bearded oaks."

Waterhouse House. Louis Sams, a planter of cotton, built this house with its graceful columns and old iron gate in 1852.

Means House. This house, which has a beautiful garden in the rear, was built about 1800 by Robert Means. The interior paneling and mantel are unchanged.

B. B. Sams House. The pillars of this house, built in the 1840's, are made of solid brick. It has its original tabby slave quarters in back.

Danner-Johnson House. This buff gray brick house was built in 1849 by Dr. John A. Johnson. Marble mantels and iron grillwork ordered from Italy were stopped by the Civil War blockade.

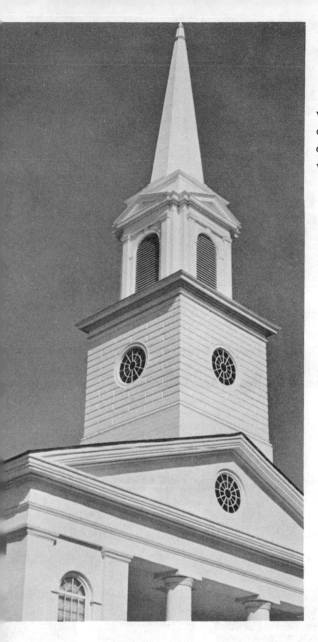

Baptist Church. This white stucco edifice with small windows has box pews. It was completed in 1844. In 1875, it had 3317 one-time slave members and only 182 whites.

St. Helena's Episcopal Church. Surrounded by a high brick wall, St. Helena's was built of brick and stucco in 1724 and is the oldest church in Beaufort. The interior has fine color detail, an elaborate cornice, and delicate balusters lining its slave balcony. The silver communion plate, given in 1734 by Captain John Ball, is still in possession of the church.

Secession House. Known also as the Edmund Rhett House, the residence was erected in 1743. Like other Beaufort houses, it has an arcaded basement with grills on the arches and a foundation of tabby. Elaborate matching cornices are seen in all rooms. The house was a hotbed of sentiment for southern independence for some years before the Civil War. Edmund Rhett was a brother of U.S. Senator Robert B. Rhett, called the father of secession.

The Anchorage. Once a hotel annex and now a guest house, the Anchorage, built of brick and stucco, was erected in 1776 by William Elliott. In addition to carved mantels, the old house boasts of four-poster beds, elaborate chandeliers, and fine old paintings. One suite of furniture is from the home of General Pierre Beauregard, one of Robert E. Lee's generals. (Open)

Tabby Manse. Thomas Fuller built this house in about 1786. An original Adam mantel and paneling remain, and a charming mahogany staircase leads to a second-floor ballroom, which has fine paneling and a carved mantel. Stucco covers the exterior walls made of tabby.

Tabby Manse. Fine carving enhances the mantel in the parlor.

Lee House. This pre-Revolutionary house, well shaded by a large live oak, is believed to have been moved to Beaufort from the Jenkins plantation on nearby St. Helena Island.

John Joiner Smith House. An elaborately carved and paneled door on the front of the house does not open. It is merely designed to enhance the façade. Access to the house is through French windows and an actual door on the side. The house was built in about 1813.

John Joiner Smith House. Under the spreading limbs of an old live oak, the opposite shore of St. Helena Bay can be seen.

Lafayette House. John M. Verdier, planter and merchant, built this house in 1795 in the heart of the downtown area, where he could see his ships at dock. The Marquise de Lafayette visited the house in 1825. It now contains offices. (Open)

Lafayette House. A second-floor ball-room is reached by this staircase, with carved step-ends, which divides under a Palladian window.

Lafayette House. This panel is seen on the ballroom mantel.

Cheraw, South Carolina

WELSHMEN FROM PENNSYLVANIA SETTLED Cheraw, located in the northeast corner of the state, in about 1752. Only 35 persons were living there in 1819, but there were more than 800 people and 250 houses by 1823 because the Big Pee Dee River had been opened up to navigation. This permitted team boats, pole boats, and steamboats to carry produce to and from other points in the two Carolinas.

Captain Moses Rogers, who in 1819 made the first trans-Atlantic crossing using steam power in the *S.S. Savannah*, lived in Cheraw and commanded a river steamer.

The large number of trees planted in as many as four rows on some streets is attributed to an old town ordinance requiring anyone seen to be intoxicated to bring and plant a tree from the woods.

An outstanding event in the little town's history occurred in 1824 when the Baptists and Presbyterians both wanted to hold services in St. David's Church. One Sunday, when the Baptists were in possession, the Presbyterians loaded and fired an old cannon that had been used in the Revolution. Consternation ensued, and the Baptist preacher dismissed his congregation and fled.

Later the Episcopalians occupied the church, and the Presbyterian preacher responsible for firing the cannon wrote ruefully: "While the lion and the unicorn were fighting for the crown, up came a puppy dog and knocked them both down."

St. David's Church. Named for the patron saint of Wales, the church was built in 1770–1773. The frame structure on the far edge of town has three arched windows in its square tower, each below a balustraded deck. The British used it as a hospital during the Revolution.

Old Market Hall. The first story of the building is made of stuccoed brick; the top is built of frame covered with clapboards. The second-story piazza juts out over the sidewalk. It was erected in 1836 as the town hall, and later became the city courthouse.

Cherokee Inn. The large brick structure built in 1833 was designed by an architect from Philadelphia for a banker who used it both as a residence and as a bank. Later it became a hostelry and then reverted to service as a bank again. (Open)

Hartsell House. This frame house built of hand-hewn lumber in about 1780 served General Sherman as his personal headquarters in 1865.

Enfield. General Erasmus Powe, who fought in the war of 1812, built this house in 1820. It has two small wings. Except for the placement of the chimneys, the central part bears a close resemblance to the Hartsell House.

Lazarus House. Major M. H. Lazarus of Charleston built this imposing house with its pedimented portico in 1825. Recently it was moved back from the street.

McKay House. This is another of the many houses in which Lafayette was entertained in 1825. It was built in 1820 and has two porticos which are almost identical. Entrance doorways with elliptical fanlights are repeated on the second floor.

Camden, South Carolina

ENGLISH FAMILIES BEGAN THE SETTLEMENT of Camden in 1733–1740 and were joined in 1750–1751 by Irish Quakers, who called their colony Friend's Neck. Later it became known as Pine Tree Hill and finally was named Camden in 1768 to honor Charles Pratt, Earl of Camden, a champion of colonial rights.

The town is located northwest of Columbia, the state capital, near the Wateree River.

After the fall of Charleston in 1780, Lord Cornwallis entered Camden and made it the principal British garrison in the state. Fourteen Revolutionary battles were fought there, the most important being the Battle of Camden in August, 1780, called the Americans' most disastrous defeat of the war. It resulted in the routing of General Horatio Gates, a British officer who had taken the side of the colonials, by Lord Rawdon and the mortal wounding of General de Kalb, the German-born officer serving in the Continental Army.

General Nathanael Greene, who superseded Gates, advanced on the town but was driven off by Rawdon's forces, who later burned and evacuated the town after raids by the local militia.

An onlooker at the events was thirteen-year-old Andrew Jackson, future President of the country, who watched from a stockade where he had been confined by the British.

Six Confederate generals were born in Camden.

Kamchatka. General James Chestnut built the house on this large estate in 1854. It later was the home of William F. Buckley.

Greenleaf Villa. Samuel Flake built the house in 1803. It later was the home of a physician, a cousin of Robert E. Lee, who used it as a Confederate hospital. It was fired by Union soldiers but saved by Mrs. Lee, who personally directed a bucket brigade.

Ivy Lodge. This dwelling, built of brick and stone on the first floor and frame on the second and third, was erected about 1780. It was the home of Dr. Simon Baruch, a surgeon in the Army of Northern Virginia and father of Bernard M. Baruch, the financier. Dr. Baruch is given credit for the development of the appendectomy.

Bethesda Presbyterian Church. This edifice was designed in 1820 by Robert Mills, prominent American proponent of Greek Revival design. The main entrance and steeple are at the rear. The floor and pews rise as they recede from the pulpit, which is placed in the front of the church. (Open)

Old Courthouse. Mills also designed this building, erected in 1826. It is made of stuccoed brick with corner pilasters. It originally had six Ionic columns, whose capitals later were used as carriage blocks when they were replaced.

Columbia, South Carolina

ALTHOUGH THE VICINITY OF COLUMBIA ON the Conagree River in the center of the state was first settled in about 1700, little came of it until the state selected Colonel Thomas Taylor's plantation, "The Plains," and nearby farms as the site of the new capital.

The legislature first convened there in 1790 in an unfinished statehouse after a stagecoach line to Charleston had been established. George Washington, who went there in the following year, described the town as "an uncleared wood with very few houses in it."

The textile industry became the first economic backbone of Columbia. South Carolina College, now the University of South Carolina, was chartered there in 1801.

At a meeting in Columbia in December, 1860, an Ordinance of Secession was drawn up to sever the state's connection with the Union, but an epidemic of smallpox caused the convention to move to Charleston, where the Ordinance finally was approved. Even so, the action caused great jubilation in Columbia when the news reached there.

Not until February, 1865, did the Civil War come to the capital. That was when Sherman's army began to shell the town from across the Conagree. When the Mayor quickly surrendered the city, Sherman is quoted as promising that "order would prevail and courtesy be shown."

Nevertheless, that same night the city found itself in flames. Destroyed were 84 city blocks on 366 acres and 1386 buildings. Of all the buildings on Main Street, only the partly completed capitol survived the conflagration. Blameless though he may have been personally, the name of General Sherman is not revered in Columbia.

A grievous period followed, with the government in the hands of carpetbaggers and scallawags, before sane government was restored.

Seibels House. A. M. Hale is believed to have erected this house in about 1796. The first story is made of brick, the second of frame. Its Georgian lines somewhat resemble those of Mount Vernon.

DeBruhl-Marshall House. John DeBruhl built this house in 1820. His widow saved it from the fire in 1865 by persuading Union soldiers to extinguish flames they had started.

144

Governor's Mansion. The mansion, situated on spacious grounds, was built in 1855 to serve as the officers' barracks for the Arsenal Academy and was the only part of the school to escape burning in 1865. Its white stucco is trimmed with green shutters.

Fisher-Bachman House. Dr. Edward Fisher built this house in 1801, but Dr. John Bachman added the ironwork, the portico, and the arched decoration over the doors and windows in the 1840's in preparation for the wedding of his daughter.

Presbyterian Church. Gothic Revival in style, the brick edifice built in 1853 is covered with reddish brown stucco. The parents of Woodrow Wilson are buried in the adjacent churchyard.

Trinity Episcopal Church. Edward B. White designed the church in 1840. Its twin towers each support eight pinnacles. The transepts were added in 1861–1862. Most of the stained glass windows are from Munich.

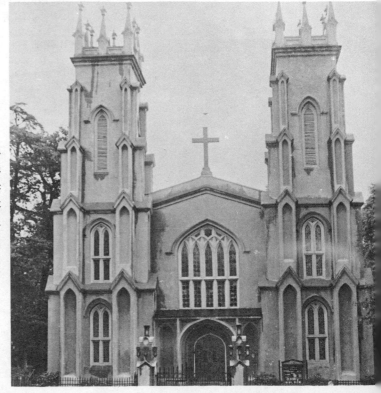

Trinity Episcopal Church. Back of the altar are five lancet windows.

Statehouse. Begun in 1851, but not roofed and first used until 1869, the structure bears the scars of Union shells. It measures 300 feet by 150 feet and is 180 feet high to the dome. The north and south entrances have 12 fluted Corinthian columns approached by monumental granite steps.

Statehouse. This is the heavily carved entrance to a legislative chamber.

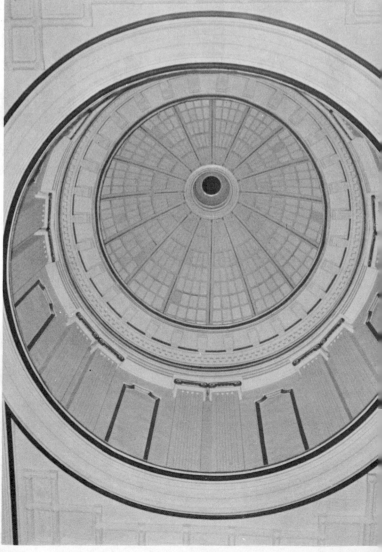

Statehouse. The interior of the high dome is impressively embellished.

148

Statehouse. A balcony runs around the second floor under the handsomely decorated interior.

Athens, Georgia

Like Chapel Hill in North Carolina, Athens was founded to be a college town. John Milledge, later governor of Georgia, donated 633 acres on the Oconee River, between Atlanta and the South Carolina border, as the site for the college, and in the fall of 1801 John Meigs, a former student at Yale University, hastily pushed the construction of a few log and frame buildings and sold lots in the new town to raise money for the institution.

Although the first permanent building was not completed until 1805, classes were held in 1801 under great oak trees, with the Cherokee Indians as interested specta-tors. The Indians did not interfere with the establishment of either the town or the college.

Named after Athens, Greece, the new town lived up to its namesake with the building of numerous classic revival homes with their Greek porticos, pediments, and Doric columns.

In 1862, aroused by the fiery eloquence and persuasiveness of Thomas R. R. Cobb, an ardent secessionist who became a general in the Confederate Army, so large a part of the student body enlisted in the southern army that the college had to close in the following year for lack of students.

Cobb House. The white frame house was built between 1830 and 1840, and the octagonal wings were added in 1843 when Thomas R. R. Cobb bought it. The new owner was the secessionist and orator. He helped greatly in bringing about Georgia's break with the Union and in drafting the new Confederate Constitution. The house now is church property.

150

J. H. Lumpkin House. This house was built in about 1845 by Joseph Henry Lumpkin, a co-founder of the Lumpkin Law School and Georgia's first Chief Justice. It later became the Home school, founded by a political refugee from Poland.

Hill House. The beautiful white clapboard house with the divided front entrance stairs has a peristyle of 14 Corinthian columns around the front and two sides. It was built in 1855 by Thomas Grant of Virginia and in 1869 came into the possession of Benjamin H. Hill, prominent Georgia statesman, who became a U.S. Congressman and Senator. The house now is the home of the president of the University of Georgia. It has splendid interior plaster cornices and ceiling medallions, crystal chandeliers, and twin marble mantels.

Grady House. This house was built in 1845 by General Robert Taylor and later rented to the mother of Henry Grady, who became managing editor of the Atlanta Constitution. Its 13 massive Doric columns are said to represent the 13 American colonies.

E. H. Lumpkin House. The brownstone house has corner quoins and a wrought-iron piazza. Built between 1845 and 1850, it now is church property. Here in 1891 was founded the first ladies' garden club in the United States.

Upson House. Distinguished by its magnificent magnolias and six tall white columns, this handsome house was built in 1840.

Phinizy House. The double porch and wrought-iron railings of this house, built in about 1857 by Ferdinand Phinizy, are suggestive of New Orleans.

Hamilton House. This ante-bellum home of J. S. Hamilton, which became a fraternity house, has wide verandas on three sides. The ironwork came from England. The house has excellent carved mantels.

Dearing House. Built in 1856, this stunning red brick house with white Doric columns extending around both sides belonged to the A. P. Dearing family until it was sold to a sorority in 1938.

Dearing House. The parlors of the house are splendidly furnished with period chairs, tables, and mirrors.

Dearing House. This exquisite secretary and the crystal chandelier are in the library.

Dearing House. The handsomely draped 24-pane windows in the drawing room extend down to the floor.

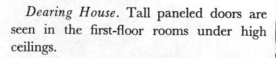

Dearing House. Tall paneled doors are seen in the first-floor rooms under high ceilings.

Dearing House. This fine old furniture is grouped in a corner of the dining room.

Mell House. Combining Victorian and Greek Revival features, this pre-Civil War house has eight narrow two-story columns.

Washington, Georgia

THIS TOWN PROUDLY BOASTS OF BEING the first in the nation to be named after George Washington, having been so named by the Executive Council of the province while the Revolution still was being fought. The first settlers—from Virginia and the Carolinas—came, starting in 1774, and erected a stockade called Ford Heard.

Colonel Elijah Clarke, after whom a state park has been named, is credited with the leadership that enabled the settlers to survive British attack in 1779. Colonel John Dooly and Colonel Andrew Pickens also were prominent. A decisive battle was fought with the British at Kettle Creek, four miles outside town, which turned back the attacking British and broke their hold in Georgia.

In 1790, a committee from the Presbyterian Church met at Washington and ordained Georgia's first Presbyterian minister, the Reverend John Springer, on a spot now commemorated by a marker.

It was in Washington, situated between Athens and Augusta, that the final cabinet meeting of the Confederacy was convened on May 5, 1865. The last papers were signed on this occasion, and the government was officially dissolved. Fourteen ranking Confederate officials were present, including President Davis.

Here also was the home of the country's first woman newspaper editor—Sarah Hillhouse. She became editor of the *Washington Monitor* in 1804.

Dugas House. A French refugee from Santo Domingo, Louis Dugas, built this house in 1800. It was the birthplace of Dr. Louis Alexander Dugas, a distinguished physician and surgeon who founded the Medical College of Georgia.

Barnett-Slaton House. Albert Gallatin Semmes, who became an Associate Justice of the Supreme Court of Florida, erected this house in about 1835. It later was the home of Samuel Barnett, attorney and author and Georgia's first Railroad Commissioner. Now a Confederate museum, the house contains an interesting collection of war and Indian relics and ante-bellum furniture. (Open)

Barnett-Slaton House. The high-backed settee rests under a fine old oval mirror in the parlor.

Barnett-Slaton House. The tall secretary and its chair fill a corner in the double parlor.

Barnett-Slaton House. The silver service is shown on an old table in front of the chair rail in the dining room.

Barnett-Slaton House. The large oval banquet table nearly fills the dining room of the house.

Randolph-Colley House. Built in the late 1700's, this was the home of Maria Randolph, a descendant of Pocahontas, who was six feet tall "and every inch a woman," according to local lore. Back of the two-column portico is a narrow hanging balcony. A ballroom extends the length of the house on the first floor.

Wickersham House. This house was built in the early 1800's as a dormitory for the Female Academy. It has interesting brass locks.

Toombs House. Dr. Joel Abbott of Connecticut built this house, starting in 1794, and in 1837 it became the home of Robert A. Toombs, statesman, lawyer, author, and Confederate general. Behind the Doric columns are French windows that open into spacious parlors. Massive iron chandeliers were brought down from Toombs' house in Washington, D.C., when he left his place in the U.S. Senate following Georgia's secession from the Union.

Presbyterian Church. The charming white church was erected in 1825 under the leadership of Alexander Hamilton Webster, who had come down from Connecticut to teach in the Female Academy. A balustrade runs around the organ in the back of the church. (Open)

Alexander House. Felix and William Gilbert of Virginia built the early part of this large brick and frame house in 1808, after having camped on the property during a hunting trip.

Gaines House. This house, built prior to 1800, once was part of the Female Academy but has been moved from its original site.

Holly Court. The oldest part of the house was built in 1825, the remainder having been built some miles away and added to the original in 1851. It was here that Mrs. Jefferson Davis awaited the arrival of her husband, who was fleeing from Union troops after the Confederacy fell. It has an excellent stairway and tall mantels.

Jordan-Lindsey House. A hanging balcony runs around the house back of the Doric colonnade. It actually is two houses joined together and has two identical front doors. It was the home of Duncan G. Campbell, author of the treaty covering removal of the Cherokee Indians from Georgia. His son, John A. Campbell, was an Associate Justice of the U.S. Supreme Court. The house, built in the early 1800's, contains interesting woodwork.

Augusta, Georgia

THE NEED FOR A TRADING POST AND PLACE of defense against Indians led to the founding of Augusta, across the Savannah River from South Carolina. As it turned out, the authorities were singularly successful in preserving peace with the Indians, and there were no serious incidents.

A highway was built to Savannah in 1740 and, with the coming of more than 100 persons to the settlement, St. Paul's Church was established in 1750.

The British occupied Augusta in 1781 during the Revolution but, after a prolonged siege, succumbed to troops led by Light Horse Harry Lee of the Continental Army.

Augusta became the state capital in 1786 and retained that distinction for ten years.

The raising of tobacco gave the town's economy new impetus after the war, but after Eli Whitney invented the cotton gin nearby in 1793 the growing of cotton received greatly increased emphasis, and cotton began to replace tobacco as the nineteenth century advanced. Steamboats and pole boats carried the cash crops to seaport down the river.

The people of the town were besieged by yellow fever from 1840 to 1854.

When the Civil War came, Augusta became the site of the Confederate powder works, so when General Sherman started his march from Atlanta to the sea the town assumed it would be destroyed. But Sherman neglected Augusta as he turned his attentions to Savannah.

High Gate. The rear portion of the house was built by slaves before 1800, and in 1838 a virtual duplicate of the original was added in front. One-story rooms connect the two sections.

Cumming-Longdon-Weiss House. The Georgian house with its wide piazza and wrought-iron railings on the second floor was built in 1826.

Montgomery Place. The square frame house, with the ornamental balcony suspended over the doorway back of the six white columns, was erected in 1830. It is now a public library. (Open)

Montgomery Place. A modest archway stands in front of the arched and paneled door in the entrance hall.

Montgomery Place. The drawing room has tasteful plasterwork in its cornice and walls.

168

Montgomery Place. The carved mantel and high overmantel are still to be seen in the drawing room.

Montrose. This yellow clapboarded house with its white Corinthian columns was built in 1849 by Robert Reid and became the home of Colonel Charles Colcock Jones. A double drawing room contains two handsome marble mantels.

Old White House. Built in 1750, this is regarded as the oldest standing house in Augusta. It was known as McKay's Trading Post during the Revolution, when British forces retreated there and were besieged by patriots until British reinforcements arrived. It has an interesting circular staircase. The house is now a museum. (Open)

Eve House. This house, built on a high brick basement in 1814, was the home of Dr. Paul F. Eve, surgeon in the Polish Army during the war of 1830. The iron balcony on the second floor overhangs the sidewalk.

Phinizy Place. The large brick house was built in 1841 and became the home of Charles Phinizy. It is distinguished for its graceful, iron-railed, horseshoe stairway that leads up to its second-floor entrance. The basement has pink marble floors and waist-high dadoes. The house now is a private club.

Presbyterian Church. The gray stucco edifice was erected in 1812 from plans by Robert Mills, designer of the Washington Monument. It has a three-tiered Georgian tower surmounted by a spire. (Open)

Medical College. Erected in 1835, the stuccoed brick building was designed by C. C. Cluskey for the Medical Academy of Georgia, the first school of medicine in the state. It now is the headquarters of a garden club.

Academy Building. The stucco-covered structure erected in 1802 originally housed the Academy of Richmond County. It became a Confederate hospital during the Civil War and of late has served as a museum and library. (Open)

Ware Mansion. The house built in 1818 by Nicholas Ware was called Ware's Folly because it cost $40,000. Lafayette was feted there at a ball. The frame residence is ornamented in Adam style and has an elliptical stairway winding up to the attic. The house has identical fan-lighted and side-lighted doorways on both the first and second floors.

Government House. Probably designed by Gabriel Manigault of South Carolina, the building was constructed in 1790 when Augusta was the state capital. George Washington was honored there by the state in 1791. The low wings of the stuccoed brick building were added later. It has white Carrara mantels and wide floor boards.

Milledgeville, Georgia

THIS TOWN WAS LAID OUT IN 1803 AS THE site of the state capital. It was named for John Milledge, Revolutionary soldier, member of the U.S. House of Representatives, governor of Georgia, and then U.S. Senator.

It is a town of wide streets and large public squares. Many of the streets were laid out to be 100 feet in width and several were twice as wide.

Federal troops previously had been stationed in the vicinity at nearby forts, at one of which was signed the treaty of 1802 in which the Indians ceded lands in the area to the state.

Here in the capitol building the Secession Convention met in January, 1861, and the secession ordinance was adopted after several days of debate.

In 1864, on his march to the sea from Atlanta, General Sherman freed the convicts and burned the penitentiary, but spared other buildings. Stores of cotton in the town were confiscated, instead of being burned as had been the case at some other captured places.

The capital was transferred to Atlanta in 1868, and the various state buildings in Milledgeville were turned to other uses.

Old State Capitol. Originally completed in 1807 at a cost of $60,000, the building with its battlemented crestings was restored after a fire in 1943. It was designed by Small and Lane.

Old Executive Mansion. Here was the home of eight governors between 1838, when it was built, and 1879. It now is the home of the president of Georgia College for Women. Designed after the Palladio, it cost $50,000. Great doors open into a square entrance hall with a parlor on one side and a library on the other. Two mantels of Italian marble remain. The rotunda back of the entrance hall rises to a height of 50 feet. (Open)

Old Executive Mansion. A massive four-poster and chandelier are prominent in a first-floor bedroom.

Old Executive Mansion. A large gilded mirror hangs over the marble mantel in the drawing room.

Old Executive Mansion. This is the interior of the rotunda as seen from the first floor.

Fort House. Built around 1800, this was the home of Tomlinson Fort, leader of the Union Party in the Georgia legislature, member of the Board of Trustees of the University of Georgia, and president of the National Bank of Georgia.

Gordon House. This frame house with the wide porches, built in 1820, once was a governor's mansion. It has excellent mantels and old furniture.

177

Orme-Crawford House. John Williams built the house in 1820 and sold it in 1836 to Richard McAllister Orme of Maryland. Back of its finely proportioned portico are two fan-lighted doorways, one opening onto a hanging balcony.

Orme-Crawford House. A handsome stairway with elaborate step-ends winds its way to the second floor.

Orme-Crawford House. Here is a closer view of the two doorways on the front of the house.

Williams-Jones-Ferguson House. Similar in size and appearance to the Orme-Crawford house across the corner, this house was built in 1817 by Peter J. Williams.

Harris House. This clapboard house with the heavy chimneys was erected in the early 1800's by Judge Iverson Louis Harris, who planted a double row of oak trees on near-by streets so that he could walk to his office in the shade.

Macon, Georgia

THE TOWN IN THE CENTER OF THE STATE was not founded by the legislature until 1823, after the Creek and Cherokee Indians had been removed, but President Thomas Jefferson had established Fort Hawkins across the Ocmulgee River in 1806 as a trading center and place for negotiating with the Indians. Thomas Tatum built a cabin opposite the fort in 1822, and the first lots were sold in the following year.

The new town is said to have been designed after the ancient city of Babylon.

Before the railroad reached Macon from Savannah in 1843, the town had become an important river port accommodating boats up to 50 tons in capacity. Its superior transportation facilities resulted in the development of an extensive trade in cotton.

In the Civil War, Macon became a depository for the Confederate Treasury and a distribution center for supplies. An arsenal was moved there and saddles, harnesses, shot, cannons, and small arms were manufactured in the town.

Macon was not seriously threatened by attack until July, 1864, when three Union raids were repulsed. However, it was surrendered in April, 1865, and Jefferson Davis was brought there after his capture and before he was removed to Fortress Monroe in Virginia.

Judge Holt House. This house, struck by a cannon ball during the Federal attack on Macon in 1864, was built in 1853 by Judge Asa Holt.

Johnston-Hay House. Started in 1855 from plans obtained in Italy by William B. Johnston, this 24-room mansion is finished with mahogany and rosewood. Among the rooms is a ballroom adorned with crystal chandeliers. Mr. Johnston was in charge of the Confederate depository in Macon.

Overlook. Located on the crest of Coleman Hill, this striking mansion has a commanding view of downtown Macon. It was completed in 1840 for Jerry Cowles, railroad builder and banker. The temple-like mansion is surrounded by a Doric colonnade, which supports an entablature ornamented by simple triglyphs on the frieze. Union General James H. Wilson lived there during the military occupation after the Civil War. It has 14 Carrara mantels and a front door with silver hinges. It now houses a private school. (Open)

Overlook. This large medallion appears
on the ceiling of a first-floor parlor.

Overlook. This free-hanging, winding
stairway with carved step-ends rises from
the entrance hall.

Overlook. This massive front door is said to weigh 500 pounds.

Overlook. Double columns support an arch on either side of the wide entrance hall.

Holt-Peeler House. Judge Thaddeus Goode Holt built this house in 1840. It was designed by Alexander Elam and is known for its horseshoe entrance steps with iron railings. Born here was his granddaughter, Nanaline Holt, who became the mother of the heiress, Doris Duke. In back of the columns is a graceful hanging balcony.

Carmichael House. The house was built in 1846 in the form of a modified Greek cross from plans published in a fashion book. Its superb winding stairway rises to a cupola above the second floor. It was the home of R. J. Carmichael.

The Columns. Originally built in 1850, the Greek Revival house with tall columns on three sides and an intricate frieze was extensively remodeled in 1895.

Carneal House. This was the large home built by Thomas Carneal, one of the charterers of the town, in 1815. The Georgian Colonial design is embellished with Italian Renaissance features. Carneal is credited with giving asylum to Negroes seeking to escape from southern Kentucky and helping them cross the Ohio River to safety.

Covington, Kentucky

SITUATED AT THE JUNCTURE OF THE OHIO and Licking Rivers, across from Cincinnati, Covington was located on a 200-acre site for which scrip had been issued to George Muse, a Virginia soldier, in return for military service in the French and Indian War.

Mr. Muse is said to have traded the scrip for a keg of whiskey in 1780. The new owner, in turn, traded it to General James Taylor for a quarter of buffalo. The general then dealt it off to Colonel Stephen Trigg, who passed it on to James Welch, who had it surveyed and then sold it to Thomas Kennedy for $750.

Kennedy made his purchase in 1801 and promptly built a large stone house near the rivers, where he lived as a tavern keeper and ferryman. Later he sold 150 acres of his holding to John S. Gano, Richard M. Gano, and Thomas Carneal, who chartered the town in 1815 and named it for General Leonard Covington, of Maryland, a hero of the War of 1812. Immediately across the Licking River to the east was a smaller town named Newport that had been settled a few years earlier than Covington.

Covington became a trading center in the 1830's, as settlers from across the Appalachians headed down the Ohio River and then through Kentucky. After them came a large German immigration.

During the Civil War, the sympathies of the people were divided, but warfare did not threaten the town, except for some brief skirmishes with Confederate pickets.

Beard House. Built in the mid-1850's, this brick house was the boyhood home of Daniel C. Beard, founder of the Boy Scouts of America after he first had formed the Sons of Daniel Boone.

Clayton House. This white frame house was built of ships' timbers in 1839 by John W. Clayton. It once housed a private school, among whose pupils was Frederick D. Grant, a son of President U. S. Grant.

Duveneck House. This simple, modernized dwelling, constructed before 1848. was the birthplace of Frank Duveneck, who started as a church decorator and then became a well-known artist, muralist, and art teacher.

Southgate House. Colonel Wright Southgate built this 20-room brick mansion in 1821 across the river, in nearby Newport, on a rise overlooking the Ohio River. It has a winding staircase and a lookout with four very small windows. It now is a private club.

Taylor Mansion. After a discontented slave had burned the first house on the site, James Taylor built this mansion in Newport in about 1837. Originally it faced the Ohio River but was remodeled so that the back became the front. It has wide halls and 16-foot ceilings. It now is a funeral parlor. (Open)

Taylor Mansion. A splendid staircase winds up through the high first floor ceiling at the side of the entrance hall.

Taylor Mansion. Corinthian columns flank the wide hall under a decorated ceiling.

Taylor Mansion. The curved front door contains delicate carving and a large stained glass panel.

Paris, Kentucky

COLONEL JOHN FLOYD FIRST SURVEYED THE town in 1776 but it was not established until 1789, although court was held there in 1786 in an old rock house known as Fairfield, and a courthouse with a jail 16 feet square was built the same year.

The town, located just a few miles northeast of Lexington, first was known as Hopewell, but was renamed Paris in appreciation of the aid the new nation had received from France during the Revolution.

Among the early records preserved in the courthouse are several suits filed against Daniel Boone for debt. Nearby Stoner Creek is named after Michael Stoner, a companion of Boone.

Pennsylvanians opened a distillery in Paris in 1790, and the town later became a large source of bluegrass seed.

The first tavern, built in 1788, which still stands near the courthouse, was Duncan Tavern. Another early hostelry built to accomodate travelers between Maysville and Lexington was the Indian Queen, erected in 1804. It has since been demolished.

William H. McGuffey, compiler of the famous readers, taught school in Paris in about 1822.

There was military activity on four occasions during the Civil War, but none of the battles was decisive. The town was under martial law frequently during the war.

The Grange. Ned Stone, a slave dealer, had the brick house built in 1818 with a dungeon under the central hall in which to confine unruly subjects. It has a deep-set doorway with a fan-light and side-lights. The slightly curved walls of the pavillions are pierced by Palladian windows. The stairway has delicate balusters, newel post, and stair rail.

Cane Ridge Meeting House. Presbyterians from North Carolina constructed the meeting house in 1791, using ash logs chinked with mud on a foundation of stone. Hand-split oak shakes four feet long covered the roof. The historic log building now is completely covered by a modern brick structure to preserve it from the elements. This was the scene of great religious revivals in the early 1800's, when the Reverend Barton W. Stone was the pastor. One gathering numbering between 20,000 and 30,000 persons assembled to hear five or more clergymen preaching simultaneously. (Open)

Woodlawn. The heavily-shaded brick house was built in about 1820 on a farm outside town.

Mt. Airy. John Hildreth built the house with its recessed wings in about 1820 and later sold it to Captain William E. Simms.

Duncan Tavern and Anne Duncan House. Major James Duncan built the 20-room tavern of rock in 1788. Oak and ash beams, girders, and joists used in the structure, which appears on the right, are still sound. It had a ballroom and billiard room. The tavern remained in continuous use until 1940, when the city presented it to the Daughters of the American Revolution, who have restored it and operate it as a museum. The widow of James Duncan tried to operate the tavern after his death in about 1800, but leased it in 1803, after building a home flush against the tavern on the left. It is made of logs clapboarded with split hickory laths and has old blue ash floors. The widow reared six children born in the tavern and raised in the house. One became a member of the U.S. House of Representatives and another was governor of Illinois. In restoring the house, materials from other old buildings were used, including facing stone from Fairfield, where the first court was held. (Open)

Duncan Tavern. The secretary stands in the Isaac Shelby room, named for the state's first governor.

Duncan Tavern. This handsomely carved mantel and overmantel are in the room named for Kentucky's second governor, James Gerrard.

Duncan Tavern. The dining room has a spacious built-in cupboard.

Duncan Tavern. In another parlor can be seen this large oval mirror in back of an early table and chair.

Richmond, Kentucky

COLONEL JOHN MILLER OF RICHMOND, Virginia, who had served at Yorktown in the Revolution, was the first settler of Richmond in 1784 and he promptly named it after his home town. He built the first house there, and the first court was held in his barn in 1798 when Richmond, situated about 30 miles southeast of Lexington, became the county seat.

John Crooke surveyed the site of the town and courthouse in 1798 after the court had purchased two acres of ground from Colonel Miller, and the sheriff was directed "to lay off the prison bounds, with the jail in the center, and to build the stocks, whipping post, and stray pen."

When the town was incorporated in 1809, Colonel Miller donated 50 acres to the trustees of the town to be surveyed and laid off into lots and streets. Lots sold for $25 to $50 each.

A log tavern was operated by Robert Miller in 1812. Kit Carson was born only three miles away. In 1850, a cholera epidemic killed 50 persons within two months and over half the population fled.

Richmond was the scene of conflict in the Civil War from early 1861 to the end of the war. Many buildings were scarred by the engagement in 1862 between General William Nelson's Union forces and General Kirby Smith's Confederates, which began six miles south of town and developed into a sharp and continuous Federal retreat through Richmond, becoming the first important Confederate victory in Kentucky. Union losses were 225–400 dead, 350-1100 wounded, and 6000 taken prisoner. The Confederate casualties were fewer than 500.

White Hall. This was the home of General Green Clay and his son, General Cassius M. Clay. It was enlarged in 1864 around the original mansion constructed in 1787, said to have been the first brick house built in the vicinity. The central portion has two and a half stories, 22 rooms, and three wide halls. General Cassius Clay was a noted abolitionist and U.S. Minister to Russia.

White Hall. Now in another Richmond home, this is one of six tall pier mirrors that used to adorn the parlors of the Clay mansion.

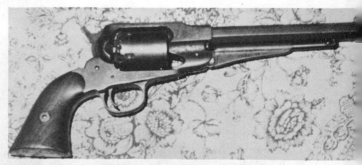

White Hall. It is said that Abraham Lincoln gave this revolver to General Cassius Clay in appreciation of his fine work in the defense of Washington during the Civil War.

Burnamwood. Built about 1830 on large, shaded grounds, this was the home of Major Curtis Field Burnam, attorney, member of the state legislature, and Assistant Secretary of the Treasury under President Grant.

Irvineton. Dr. A. W. Rollins built this large house early in the 1820's, and it came into the possession of David Irvine in 1829. Much later, his daughter gave it to the Kentucky Medical Society to be used as a hospital. It now stands in a public park.

Madison County Courthouse. Completed in 1849, this second courthouse is on the site of John Miller's barn where the first court was held. The pedimented Doric portico is surmounted by a tall domed clock tower having two octagonal stages. (Open)

Mt. Zion Church. The little brick church with its two entrances was built in 1852. The Battle of Richmond began here, and the church was struck by a cannon ball but not seriously damaged. Many Union soldiers were first buried nearby after the battle.

Woodlawn. Colonel William Rodes, de-gner of the present courthouse, whose wife as a daughter of General Cassius Clay, uilt the brick mansion in 1822. A small alustraded porch is flanked by four Palla-ian windows, two on each side. Cupboards n either side of the mantel in a back parlor ave exquisitely carved semi-circular head-gs. A carved arch spans the front hall, pported by two columns. Scenic wall-aper from the front parlor was sold for 5000 in 1923. Both sides occupied the ansion during the Civil War.

Lexington, Kentucky

THE BLUEGRASS TOWN, WHICH IS 90 MILES south of Cincinnati, was named after the battle of Lexington by Robert Patterson, Simon Kenton, and others who camped there in 1775 while on the way to build a fort near the Kentucky River. The town actually was founded in 1779, and the town plan was adopted in 1781.

In 1784, General James A. Wilkinson, a friend of George Washington, opened a store, and James Bray opened the first tavern a year later.

Transylvania Seminary, now a college, moved there from Danville in 1787. Henry Clay later was a professor in its law college.

Lexington was an important industrial town in the early 1800's until industries began to move up to the Ohio River. The breeding and training of light horses has been a principal occupation of the commu-nity ever since. Hemp for rope and tobacco were the principal agricultural crops.

Henry Clay and Confederate General John Hunt Morgan are among the more famous sons of Lexington, which also was the childhood home of Mary Todd, wife of Abraham Lincoln.

John Filson, Kentucky's first historian, conducted a private academy there until his death in 1788.

The new government of the state of Kentucky met in Lexington in 1792. The legislature met in a capitol built of logs, the Sheaf of Wheat Tavern, which served as a temporary statehouse.

The University of Kentucky, which is located at Lexington, did not come into being until 1866, after the passage of the Morrill Land-Grant College Act.

Morrison College. Located on the Transylvania College campus and designed by Gideon Shryock, the massive building was completed in 1833. Its two-story Doric portico with fluted columns is approached by a broad flight of steps. (Open)

Gratz House. This brick house was built in 1806 for Mrs. Mary G. Maton and later became the home of Benjamin Gratz. Its wide-arched doorway and the wrought-iron railing on the entrance stoop are two interesting features.

Hunt-Morgan House. John Wesley Hunt, grandfather of General Morgan, built this magnificent gray brick house in about 1814. Hunt, a merchant and hemp grower, is said to have been the first millionaire in the West. General Morgan was killed in 1864 at Greeneville, Tennessee, after escaping from a Federal prison in Columbus, Ohio, and paying a last visit to his boyhood home in Lexington. This later was the home of Thomas Hunt Morgan, Nobel Prize winner in genetics. (Open)

Hunt-Morgan House. General Morgan's secretary-desk and its chair are in a first-floor parlor.

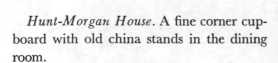

Hunt-Morgan House. A fine corner cupboard with old china stands in the dining room.

Hunt-Morgan House. A graceful circular staircase with carved step-ends winds up to the third floor from one end of the entrance hall.

Hunt-Morgan House. Unusual, folding, inside shutters are seen back of the sidelight by the front entrance.

Hunt-Morgan House. This is a close view of the exquisite entrance with its double fan-light, side-lights, and double-paneled doors.

Hunt-Morgan House. In the stable, long untenanted, are the old saddles and other gear once so often used by the General.

Hunt-Morgan House. In the lovely garden is the old privy, which has been moved forward from back in the lot. It now serves as a summer house.

Ridgely House. This home of Dr. Frederick Ridgely was built in 1794 and is regarded as a fine example of western colonial architecture.

Mary Todd Lincoln House. This is where the wife of Abraham Lincoln lived as a child. The red brick dwelling was built in the early 1800's.

Botherum House. This low house was built in the 1850's for Major Madison C. Johnson. It has four entrances, one on each side. White Corinthian columns support low porticos on each facade of the one-story house.

Rose Hill. John Brand, a hemp manufacturer, built this house in 1818, copying the entrance after that of the Temple of Minerva at Nîmes, France.

Whitehall. Gideon Shryock also designed this handsome house built in 1834–1836 for the Wear family. Thomas Marshall, a descendant of Chief Justice John Marshall, later lived here, and afterward it became the home of Mayor Claudius Johnson, whose wife, Rose Vertner, was the well-known bluegrass poet.

Pope House. John Pope, who built the red brick house soon after 1812, was a U.S. Senator and a strong opponent of Henry Clay. Here he entertained President Monroe and General Andrew Jackson.

Ashland. This is the site of the home lived in by Henry Clay, a member of the U.S. Senate at the age of twenty-nine and Speaker of the House of Representatives and Secretary of State. The original house was built in 1806 but was damaged in an earthquake, as a result of which it was taken down and rebuilt of the same materials in 1857. Benjamin Latrobe was the original architect. It has one-story wings and a main entrance that projects in the form of a bay, with a Palladian window above and a small eave pediment. A garden behind the house was planned by Pierre L'Enfant, the French landscapist who laid out the plan for the downtown District of Columbia. (Open)

Waveland. This was the home of the Bryan family, having been built in 1847 by Joseph Bryan, Sr. The University of Kentucky purchased the property in 1956 for the purpose of creating a Kentucky Life Museum, which is open to the public. It has large, splendidly furnished rooms and high ceilings, with excellent furniture and decorations ranging from early Kentucky days through the empire period. (Open)

Waveland. The cabinet containing rare old china stands in the Bryan dining room at the head of the Duncan Phyfe table.

Waveland. The secretary, topped by its broken pediment, is seen in another parlor.

Waveland. The pianoforte, said to have come from the family home of the Lees at Stratford, Virginia, is placed in the Volney Hewitt parlor.

212

Waveland. These are the former slave quarters of the old plantation.

Frankfort, Kentucky

THE FIRST WHITE MAN TO ENTER THE Frankfort region was Christopher Gist, who passed through there in 1751. Nineteen years later Daniel Boone killed an Indian warrior within the present city limits.

In 1773, Governor Dunmore of Virginia sent a survey party led by Robert McAfee, which surveyed and claimed some 600 acres, including the site of the modern capitol. In the fall of that year, adventurers came and squatted in crude shelters. The Indians resisted them and attacked, and Virginia had to send militia to restore peace and protect the settlers.

The town, which is bisected by the Kentucky River, was first named Frank's Ford, after a frontiersman who was killed there by Indians.

The Virginia legislature established the town in 1786 on 100 acres owned by General James Wilkinson and also established a ferry. Frankfort was selected as the capital in 1792 shortly after statehood was attained, because it lay between its two chief rivals for the honor—Lexington and Louisville.

The railroad came in 1835, and the town became active in livestock and lumbering and in distilling whiskey.

The Confederates seized the town in 1862, the only time the war came to Frankfort. General Braxton Bragg's forces came and set up a Confederate state government, but soon withdrew under Federal attack.

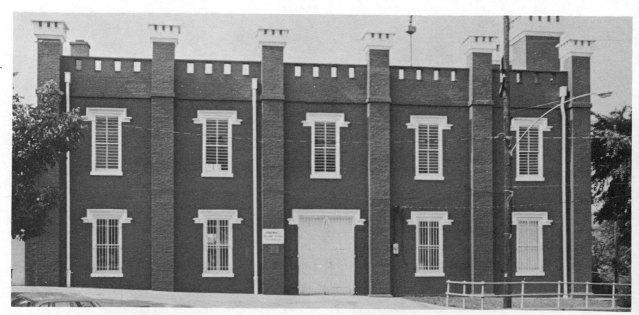

The State Arsenal. The dark green building with its battlements and turrets was built above the river in 1850 as a storehouse for the equipment and materials of the state militia.

Old Governor's Mansion. Built in 1798, this modest "palace" as it then was called was occupied by Kentucky's governors for 113 years, two of them having worked on its construction as laborers. Its 24-paned windows and attractive entrance are its best features. It has been restored as a residence and is open as a museum. (Open)

The Old Capitol. Gideon Shryock designed and built the edifice in 1827–1830 after two earlier structures had burned. It is built of marble from nearby quarries. It cost $85,000 and was used for eight decades. The front facade is dominated by a hexastyle portico of Ionic order. The columns are four feet in diameter and 33 feet high. The cupola is a pedestal 25 feet square, on which stands a circular lantern 22 feet in diameter. (Open)

Liberty Hall. This was the home of John Brown, first U.S. Senator from Kentucky, who occupied it in 1796. Its high-ceiled rooms were heated by huge fireplaces. The house contains fine mantels and other excellent woodwork. There is a ballroom on the second floor. The house has had many distinguished visitors, including Presidents Jackson, Taylor, and Theodore Roosevelt, and also Lafayette. It now is a museum. (Open)

Brown House. Shryock also designed this house, built in 1835 for Orlando Brown, second son of Senator John Brown. The design for the front façade was taken from a plan for an English country house. Brown was proud of the fact that the new house to be occupied by his young wife had, next to her room, a closet with shelves and pegs for hanging things. (Open)

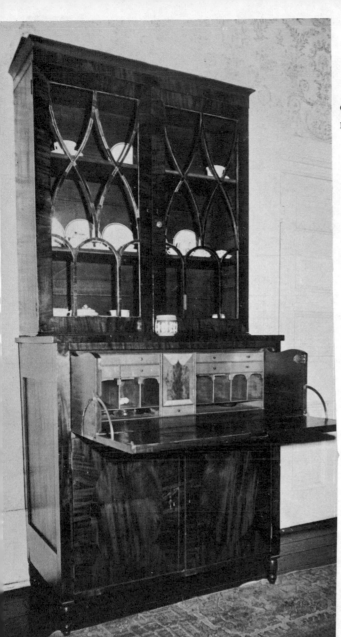

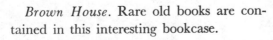

Brown House. Rare old books are contained in this interesting bookcase.

Brown House. The fine secretary is one of the many excellent pieces of family furniture in the house.

Brown House. The old kitchen fireplace and utensils seem ready for use any time they are needed.

Morehead House. Mark Hardin, registrar of the Kentucky Land Office, built this brick house in 1810. It later became the home of Kentucky Governor Charles S. Morehead.

Crittenden House. Built prior to 1821, this was the residence of John J. Crittenden, Governor of Kentucky, U.S. Congressman and Senator, U.S. Attorney General, and author of the *Crittenden Compromise*.

Louisville, Kentucky

FIRST KNOWN AS "FALLS OF THE OHIO" because of its location on that river, Louisville finally was named in honor of Louis XVI and the French nation for their aid to the American Revolution.

Two thousand acres were surveyed in 1773 by Captain Thomas Bullitt, who was commissioned by Lord Dunmore, governor of Virginia, and a patent for the land was issued to Dr. John Connally by the British Crown for his services in the French and Indian War. Then the land was confiscated by Virginia before it had been settled, because a joint owner, Captain John Campbell, was charged with being a Tory.

In 1778, George Rogers Clark with 150 volunteers came down the Ohio River from Pennsylvania and built a fort near the falls. In 1780, 300 settlers arrived, and Colonel George Slaughter with 150 men came from Virginia to protect the community.

Indians attacked the settlement in 1781, and in 1781–1782 Fort Nelson was built on the Ohio shore, across the river, as a headquarters for Clark. By 1800, there were 600 people in Louisville. John James Audubon lived there from 1808 to 1812.

From 1820 to 1870, the town's prosperity was dependent on and measured by its heavy river boat traffic. A fire in 1840 burned a large part of the business district.

Charles Dickens, the author, went to Louisville in 1842 and praised the hotel accommodations.

In the Civil War, the predominant Union sentiment of the city clashed with the pro-Confederate sympathies of the adjacent rural areas, but the city became a military headquarters for the Armies of the North.

Locust Grove. This recently restored plantation home was built in about 1790 by William and Lucy Croghan on 693 acres, one tract of which was purchased from James and Dolly Madison. Croghan, a farmer and businessman, had come to Kentucky with George Rogers Clark as deputy surveyor. The house contains rare poplar and walnut paneling, original period brass and iron locks, and excellent portraits and furniture. Presidents Monroe, Jackson, and Taylor, and local Indian chiefs were visitors at the Croghan home. (Open)

Jefferson County Courthouse. The limestone structure, designed by Shryock, was begun in 1838. In the center of the rotunda is a life-size statue of Henry Clay by Joel T. Hart. (Open)

Bank of Louisville. This dressed limestone building, also designed by Shryock, was built in 1837. Within is an elliptical dome and skylight supported by four classical columns and at either end a tapered pylon.

Christ Church. The edifice was constructed in 1822 after plans by Graham and Ferguson. Originally it had been a two-story structure, almost square, with two tiers of windows, but later it was extended and the tower was added. (Open)

Farmington. John Speed, who came ove[r] the wilderness road from Virginia in 1782 built the 14-room mansion in 1810, fron[m] plans drawn by Thomas Jefferson. The por[-] tico has an elliptical window in its pedi[-] ment. The doorway is ornamented on eac[h] side with reeded pilasters and has side-light[s] and a segmented, arched fan-light. Th[e] wide central hallway opens into two larg[e] front parlors and two octagonal room[s] behind them. The first-floor ceilings are 1[?] feet high. The land grant, signed by Patric[k] Henry, as governor of Virginia, is on di[s-] play. (Open)

Farmington. One of the octagonal rooms is furnished as a music room.

Farmington. Splendid old furniture, china, and glassware are on display in the dining room.

Farmington. The secretary with its quill pens stands in a parlor.

Farmington. A cradle and trundle bed add interest to the bedroom with its tall four-poster.

East Family Wash Shop. The main pa[r] was built about 1825, the wing later. Th[e] washing was done by horse power and th[e] ironing by weights and rollers, without ap[-]plication of heat.

Shakertown, Kentucky

Known also as the Shaker Village of Pleasant Hill, Shakertown began in 1805 when three Mercer County farmers accepted the doctrines of Mother Ann Lee, the founder of Shakerism. The first Shakers gathered in 1806 on a 140-acre Shawnee Run farm donated by Elisha Thomas. Two years later, the site of the present village, southwest of Lexington, was acquired and laid out.

A ministry led by Father John Meacham and Mother Lucy Smith arrived in 1809 to model the colony after the mother society in New Lebanon, New York. The village developed rapidly. A meeting house, shops, and barns were built, new communal families were formed, and a saw mill, fulling mill, grist mill, tannery, and other manufactories were put in operation.

In 1814, the Shakers signed the Church Covenant, dedicating their time, talents, and possessions to a faith that demanded celibate purity, separation from the world, confession of sins, and community of goods. Pleasant Hill by 1820 was prosperous and self-sufficient, and had nearly 500 members. Its plantation later was increased to over 4500 acres.

Most noted for their celibacy and religious dances, the Shakers nonetheless developed a significant way of life characterized by order, industry, benevolence, and concern for the common welfare. Their utilitarian culture found expression in the agricultural and mechanical arts. They led the state in scientific farming, propagating new breeds of sheep, hogs, and cattle and testing agricultural implements.

The society declined after the 1850's. The policy of adopting orphan children to keep up their ranks, begun during a cholera epidemic in 1834, had failed. The Civil War destroyed the southern plantation markets and, plagued by spiritual decay and financial ineptitude, the society sank deeply into debt. Membership fell from 385 in 1869 to about 100 twenty years later, while a disastrous law suit in 1896 forced them to mortgage over 3300 acres of land. In 1910, the Shaker venture came to an end when 12 old Believers turned over their remaining property to a friend in return for his perpetual care.

The village now is being restored with the aid of Federal funds.

East Family Dwelling House. One of the largest of all the buildings remaining today in Shakertown, the brick house was erected in 1817 and housed one of the five communal families.

East Family Brethren's Shop. This workshop of the brethren was built in 1845. Here they manufactured broom handles, packaged and boxed garden seeds, and printed labels and catalogs for goods to be sold.

Trustees' Office. This building, the only one in the village with any elaboration in a decorative way, was erected in 1839. It is where the trusteees, trading deacons, and office deaconesses lived.

Trustees' Office. This view of the circular stairway was taken from the first floor.

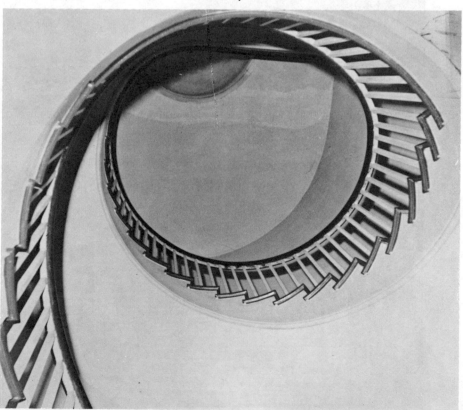

Water House. This waterworks, built in 1833, is believed to be the first put up in any Kentucky town.

Center Family Dwelling House. This large stone structure, built in 1824 and enlarged in 1834, has been converted into a splendid museum. To accommodate the celibate inhabitants, each dwelling had two entrances, dual stairways, and a wide common hall on each floor to separate the brothers' and sisters' rooms. (Open)

Center Family House. A plain but utilitarian cabinet shows the variety of medicines available to the Shakers.

Center Family House. The dining-room furniture is simple but sturdy.

Center Family House. This is one of the plain school desks and benches used by the orphan children adopted by the Shakers.

Center Family House. This is the spartanly furnished bedroom of one of the Sisters.

Center Family House. This plain desk with its pigeon-holes is quite a contrast to the elaborate secretaries seen in other old homes.

Farm Deacon's Shop. Built in 1809, this was the first permanent building in the village. In 1817, it was used as a tavern to accommodate visitors.

Old Stone Shop. Originally built as a residence in 1811, this building was used as a workshop and then, after the Civil War, became a medical office for the village physician and dentist.

West Family Dwelling House. Living in this house, built in 1821, was an older group, set apart so they might engage in tasks requiring less physical energy.

Harrodsburg, Kentucky

THE FIRST PERMANENT WHITE SETTLEMENT in Kentucky was made in Harrodstown (now Harrodsburg) just west of the upper Kentucky River, 30 miles southwest of Lexington.

In 1774, assisted by Daniel Boone, James Harrod and 31 other men laid out the settlement and built cabins, but the Indians went on the war path and drove them all away. Harrod and 30 more men returned the following year and built a palisaded fort and village. Women and children arrived the next year.

George Rogers Clark, prominent frontiersman, came in 1775 and soon became the leader of the town.

Harrodsburg was the county seat through the Revolution with a population of 198 persons, of whom 81 were eligible for military duty.

The first school in the state was conducted at the fort in 1778, and the first court held in Kentucky convened in a blockhouse at Fort Harrod in 1781. The first corn in the state was grown at Harrodsburg, and it had the first woolen mill and grist mill. Textiles were manufactured there, and flax, hemp, and tobacco were the money crops in the early years.

The Civil War ended a period of considerable prosperity, when the liberation of the slaves resulted in the impoverishment of the plantations, and the livestock and horses were requisitioned for the military. Postwar recovery was quite gradual.

Diamond Point. The deep Doric portico of this narrow house built in the 1840's protects long French windows and a richly carved doorway. The iron balcony across the facade has diamond-shaped tracery.

Doricham. A Palladian window sits above the handsome side-lighted entrance of this ante-bellum house whose pillars are well shaded.

Rykon. The widely spaced columns of this pre-Civil War house stand in front of a recessed balcony.

Morgan Row. This series of joined brick buildings in downtown Harrodsburg was built between 1807 and 1836 and operated as an inn by John Chiles, innkeeper and stagecoach operator of the 1830's. Restoration has been undertaken by the local Historical Society. (To be open)

Mansion Museum. Major James Taylor built this house near the fort in 1830. It contains Lincolniana, Confederate battlefield relics, and a music room with rare instruments. There also is a George Rogers Clark room containing prints and papers concerning his exploits. (Open)

Lincoln Marriage Cabin. This log cabin in which Thomas Lincoln and Nancy Hanks were married in 1806 has been moved from its original site at Beech Fork Settlement. It is seen within a red brick temple built to protect it. (Open)

Old Fort Harrod. This is a realistic reconstruction of the original 264-foot-square fort with blockhouses at two corners and a palisade of logs 12 feet high. The first white child born in Kentucky was born here. (Open)

Clay Hill. This large, red brick mansion erected in 1812 by Beriah Magoffin, father of a Kentucky governor, has handsome carved mantels and other woodwork. In the rear is a unique columned loggia. It sits on a gentle rise back from the street.

Aspen Hall. This large white house of great charm, built by Dr. James Shannon, president of Bacon College in 1840, now is dedicated to guests and antiques. A later occupant was Dr. Brown who founded the University of Kentucky. It stands above the street at the end of a winding lane. (Open)

Aspen Hall. A grouping of old furniture is seen in a corner of the drawing room.

Aspen Hall. A drop-leaf table and two charming side chairs rest close to the stairway with its impressive newel post and carved step-ends.

Aspen Hall. This handsome china cabinet holds a collection of old silver.

Aspen Hall. An unusually tall old secretary graces one of the parlors.

Beaumont Inn. This red brick mansion with its six-column white portico was erected in 1840 and was the home of Daughters College. It has three large parlors. (Open)

Beaumont Inn. A tall gilt-frame mirror and plush chair adorn one of the parlors.

Beaumont Inn. In a hallway are a grandfather clock and an armchair with a carved back.

Fair Oaks. Interesting designs stand out on the second-floor extremes of the antebellum brick house.

Danville, Kentucky

PIONEERS VISITED THE DANVILLE AREA, A few miles southwest of Harrodsburg, in 1774, and there was some settlement in 1776. In 1785, it became the first capital of the Kentucky District of the Commonwealth of Virginia.

Two years before that, however, there was agitation for separating Kentucky from Virginia, and Kentucky's first political club was formed in Danville at that time. In the years that followed, nine constitutional conventions were held in Danville, with the result that, in 1792, Kentucky became a state with Danville as its first capital. It is named for Walker Daniel, who obtained the deed for the town in 1784.

Also in 1792, the first post office west of the Alleghenies was established in Danville.

Even in its early days, the town was a center of culture. Transylvania College, later moved to Lexington, had been established there in 1783, Centre College followed in 1819, and the Kentucky School for the Deaf, the first school of its kind in the world to be operated at government expense, was founded there in 1823. The first law school in the West also was located at Danville.

Centre College has contributed two former vice presidents of the United States and a Chief Justice of the U.S. Supreme Court —Fred Vinson. Danville also was the home of Joseph H. Davies, who first prosecuted Aaron Burr for treason in 1807.

Caldwell Home. Jeremiah Clemens built this house out in the countryside for his daughter, Elizabeth, in 1823. A spacious front porch is formed by recessing the central portion of the façade. It was built of limestone, stuccoed, and painted white.

Nelson-Guerrant-Curry House. This is another country home, built in about 1818. Its wings, which stand forward, have simple Palladian windows.

Nelson-Guerrant-Curry House. This is the interior of the fan-lighted front entrance.

Nelson-Guerrant-Curry House. A hand-carved mantel sits back of the interesting dining-room table, above which is a crystal chandelier.

Nelson-Guerrant-Curry House. A built-in cabinet next to a drawing-room fireplace has a decorated, semi-circular top.

Yeiser House. This brick house, covered with plaster, was built in the early 1800's. The central unit is older than the wings. Located on extensive grounds, this was the home of Philip Yeiser and later of a banker named Kinnard.

First Post Office. The first post office in the West was established in a corner of this log house in 1792. General Thomas Barbee was the first postmaster. The cabin has been moved to a park, where it stands along with other old buildings.

The Pillory. Here is where persons found guilty of wrongful acts were placed on public display, with their head and hands placed through the holes in the elevated pillory.

First Meeting House. The old meeting house, which also has been moved to the park in Constitution Square, was built about 1780. It has been restored.

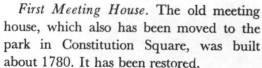

McDowell House. In this house, which was his home, Dr. Ephraim McDowell in 1809 performed the first ovariotomy (without aid of anesthesia). The house, built in about 1795, was given to the Kentucky State Medical Society as a memorial to Dr. McDowell. The clapboarded dwelling has 24-paned windows.

Bardstown, Kentucky

After having first been named Salem, the town 40 miles southeast of Louisville was renamed for William Baird (or Bard) of Pennsylvania, one of the owners of a 100-acre tract on which the town was laid out. It was incorporated by the Virginia legislature in 1778.

An early institution of learning, Salem Academy, was established there in 1788 by James Priestly.

The town has a monument to John Fitch who died there in 1798. Fitch had been a brass and silversmith and a sutler to the Continental Army during the Revolution. With the profits from the latter enterprise, he set about inventing a steamship and launched his first vessel in 1787. When his fourth ship was wrecked by a storm, his backers became discouraged and withdrew their support, so he moved to Kentucky to claim lands there.

Louis Philippe, Duke of Orleans and later King of France, spent the night in the tavern of Captain Bean near Bardstown in 1797 on a trip to New Orleans and is believed by some to have resided in Bardstown briefly and to have given lessons in French and dancing to local children.

Federal Hill. This house, which now is in a state park, owes its renown to the fact that Stephen Foster is believed to have written "My Old Kentucky Home" there while a guest of his cousin, John Rowan, Jr. The first part of the house was built in 1795 on a 1300-acre plantation by John Rowan, Sr., and it was enlarged in about 1818. Foster spent his honeymoon there and made numerous other visits to the house, which has seven large rooms 22 feet square, 15-foot ceilings, and walls 13 inches thick. All doors are Christian panels in the shape of a cross. The central hall is spanned by an arch with fluted colonettes, and all rooms have excellent mantels. (Open)

Federal Hill. The old kitchen fireplace
still has its crane and kettles.

Federal Hill. Perhaps this room is where
Stephen Foster composed his famous song.

Federal Hill. The graceful parlor mantel sits under fine old candlesticks and bold wallpaper.

Wickland. Proud to be known as the home of three governors, Wickland was built by one of them in 1813 from plans drawn by John Marshall Brown and John Rogers. The three governors were: the builder of the mansion, Charles A. Wickliffe, who was governor of Kentucky; Robert Charles Wickliffe, governor of Louisiana; and John Cripps Wickliffe Beckham, governor of Kentucky. It has a graceful stairway rising from the entrance hall. The house contains 14 rooms, five doorways, and excellent woodwork. (Open)

Talbot Tavern. The hostelry was built in 1800 and has operated ever since. An upstairs room, possibly a ballroom at one time, is decorated with murals. Next to it is The Old Stone Inn, which claims to be even older. (Open)

Rogers House. The red brick dwelling, now a funeral parlor, was erected in 1830 by John Rogers, a Baltimore architect who helped design Wickland.

Hardin House. This large red brick house was built in 1819 by Ben Hardin, a renowned criminal lawyer and a colorful character nicknamed "kitchen knife," because he was so sharp.

Old Strong House. Dr. Joseph C. Strong, who built the house prior to 1800, was surgeon on the *U.S.S. Trumbull* during the Revolution. The house contains excellent carved mantels and cornices and a free-standing staircase built by workmen imported from New England. It now is used by the Volunteers of America. (Open)

Knoxville, Tennessee

CAPTAIN JAMES WHITE OF THE CONTI-
nental Army built a log cabin in 1786,
becoming the first white settler of Knoxville. He then added three more cabins and
connected them all with a palisade of logs.

The town, which is located on the Tennessee River in the eastern end of the state,
was named for Major General Henry
Knox, Secretary of War.

The early settlers came from North
Carolina and Virginia, intent on establish-
ing a trading center. The town became a
frontier jumping-off place and gained a
reputation as a rowdy resort of teamsters,
flatboaters, soldiers, and western-bound
immigrants.

An Indian scare was averted in 1793,
when a war party killed 13 persons eight
miles away but did not attack the settlement.

A wagon road to Nashville was completed in 1795. Knoxville was the capital of
the state from 1796 until 1812, when the
capital was moved to Nashville, which is
more centrally located.

The Confederate Army occupied the
town in 1861 and arrested 1500 Union
sympathizers, but it withdrew in 1863 to be
mobilized at Chattanooga, and Major
General Burnside's army came in. The Confederates laid siege to the town and enormous property damage was experienced
before the siege was lifted some days later.
As the town recovered rapidly after the
Civil War, the population trebled between
1860 and 1870.

Park House. The gray brick, L-shaped house was begun by John Sevier, first governor of Tennessee, in 1798. Due to financial reverses, it was completed by James Park, who later became Mayor of Knoxville.

Blount Mansion. This was the first frame house west of the Alleghenies, having been built in 1792 by Governor William Blount. Its large first-floor rooms have hand-carved mantels, chair rails, and wide paneled doors. In the house are a large illuminated English Bible and Prayer Book combined, dated 1751, and a large secretary-desk that belonged to the family of Thomas Jefferson. (Open)

Blount Mansion. Handsome furniture, including the Jefferson secretary, graces the large parlor of the old mansion.

Blount Mansion. The tall-back chairs and wood-paneled walls are special features of this well-equipped early kitchen.

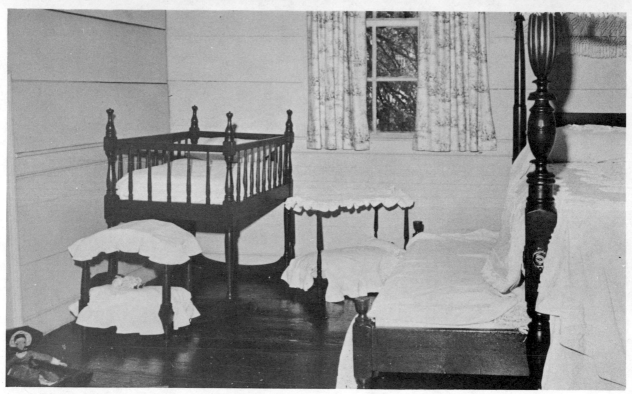

Blount Mansion. Beds for everyone—adults, children, babies, and dolls—are grouped in this second-floor bedroom.

Blount Mansion. More horizontal wall paneling is seen in another bedroom, along with a fireplace and four-poster bed.

Bleak House. This ante-bellum mansion has 15 spacious rooms and wide halls. It was built by Robert H. Armstrong and named for Charles Dickens' then popular novel. The mansion was the headquarters of Confederate General James Longstreet and his staff during the siege of Knoxville and was damaged by enemy fire. The mansion, which is adorned by a cupola, has been converted into a Confederate memorial and is furnished with relics of the Civil War and of early southern life. (Open)

Gallatin, Tennessee

THOMAS SHARPE SPENCER, WHO WAS ALmost seven feet tall and weighed over 300 pondo, was the first settler in the vicinity of Gallatin, located near the Kentucky line northeast of Nashville. He spent his first winter there in 1776 living in a hollow sycamore tree, as did early settlers of Berryville, Virginia.

After laying claim to four tracts of land, he learned he could keep only one, so he chose an 800-acre tract on the edge of the present town of Gallatin. Since then the land has been known as Spencer's Choice. He was killed by Indians.

James Trousdale, a soldier of the Revolution, was the original owner of the land on which the early town was located, having acquired it in about 1780.

The area was infested with hostile Indians at the time. They commenced their heaviest attacks on the white settlers in 1784, and the trouble continued until 1789.

The General Assembly of the state of Tennessee in 1801 appointed a commission to lay out a town for a seat of justice to be called Gallatin, and the commissioners purchased 42¼ acres from James Trousdale for $490. The town was surveyed and plotted and the sale of lots begun in 1802.

Situated on a branch of Station Camp Creek north of the Cumberland River, the town was named after Albert Gallatin, Secretary of the Treasury under Presidents John Adams and Thomas Jefferson. Early settlers had known of him as an honest and friendly merchant in Pennsylvania and wanted a town that would develop along those lines.

The Union Army first occupied the town in 1862, but it later was captured by General John Hunt Morgan of the Confederate Army. General Rosencrans of the Union Army returned later that year, and General Payne and his troops captured the town, which remained in the hands of Federal forces until after the close of the war.

Trousdale Place. This house was built in the early 1800's on the tract of land granted to James Trousdale. Later it was the home of General William Trousdale, who served in the Indian wars and at the Battle of New Orleans. He also was the 13th governor of Tennessee.

Trousdale Place. Unusual brick and stone work caps the windows of this early home.

Spencer's Choice. Colonel David Shelby built this stone residence in 1798 on the tract chosen by Thomas Spencer. Its walls are two feet thick. Its doorways and windows are set in deep paneled embrasures, and the interior has paneling and wainscoting. The house later belonged to General Joseph Miller, who introduced bluegrass to that part of the state.

Rosemont. This brick house with its recessed galleries, built in 1828, had a carriage house, smokehouse, ice house, slave house, and detached kitchen.

Cragfont. General James Winchester, an officer in the Revolution and Brigadier General in the War of 1812, built Cragfont in 1802, using stone masons and ships' carpenters brought through the wilderness from Maryland. The ballroom on the second floor has galleries on each side from which can be seen the rolling countryside. The T-shaped house is built of gray limestone. Andrew Jackson, Aaron Burr, and Lafayette were guests there. (Open)

Cragfont. Handsome paneling is seen over this delicately carved mantel in the parlor.

Cragfont. A trundle bed and seldom-seen bedsteps accompany this four-poster bed.

Fairview. Situated at the end of a long lane, this large house was built in 1832 by Isaac Franklin, who owned large tracts of land in Texas, Louisiana, and Mississippi. It once was regarded as the finest country house in Tennessee. The central hall is flanked by large-ceiled rooms. The garden façade is the same as the front. Both front and rear entrances are surmounted by beautiful fan-lights.

Foxland Hall. Thomas Baker built t Greek Revival house in 1825. The attra tive entrance has fan-lights and side-ligh The house has a fine garden known for t wide variety of its imported plants.

Duncruzin. This house erected in 1803 has a pair of bronze chandeliers from the parlors of a home of Jefferson Davis.

Nashville, Tennessee

JAMES ROBERTSON, CALLED THE FATHER of Tennessee by Andrew Jackson, led the first settlers to Nashville. He and a party built cabins and planted corn in Sulphur Bottom by the Cumberland River in 1779. Other settlers came later that year, and in 1780, both overland and by a flotilla of 30 flatboats under the supervision of Colonel John Donelson.

The legislature of North Carolina set aside 250 acres in 1784 on the site of Fort Nashborough, near the center of the state, for a new town which was called Nashville.

The Chickamaugua Indians sent strong raiding parties against the new settlement until they were crushed by an expedition led by Major James Ore. By 1790, Nashville had become a trade and manufacturing center with mills, foundries, and gun smithies supplying frontier traders and settlers.

The first steamboat coming on the Cumberland River in 1818 started a profitable era of river trade, and the town became a major shipping center for cotton. It did not become the state capital until 1843.

Although the sympathies of most of the people were with the Confederacy, the city was surrendered to Federal skirmishers in 1862, when Andrew Johnson, then a U.S. Senator from Tennessee, was appointed military governor and the town was placed under martial law. Late in 1864, the Confederates under General Thomas Hood came up from the south but, after intermittent skirmishes in the rain and snow, were crushed by the Federal defenders of the capital.

State Capitol. The imposing structure on the crest of a hill was completed in 1855. It was modeled after the Erechtheum at Athens with pedimented Ionic porticos. The east and west porticos have six Ionic columns surrounded by parapets. The structure was designed by William Strickland and follows the general plan of an Ionic temple. (Open)

St. Mary's Church. The gray brick edifice, also designed by Strickland, was completed in 1847. Its cupola is designed in the manner of the choragic monument of Lysicrates. (Open)

Presbyterian Church. Strickland also designed this church, completed in 1838. Its towers are 104 feet high, and the auditorium is decorated in the manner of an Egyptian temple. (Open)

Belmont. Colonel J. A. S. Acklen built this large mansion in 1850 in the style of an Italian Renaissance villa, with wrought-iron balconies and window guards imported from Italy. It later became a part of two educational institutions. (Open)

Belmont. Dark patterned glass lights appear over the unusual paneled doors leading from the drawing room.

Belmont. A tall, three-part mirror tops this graceful marble mantel.

Belmont. The drawing room is richly decorated with an intricate cornice.

Belmont. The handsome stairway divides as it nears the second floor.

Sunnyside. Mrs. Jesse Benton built the central frame part of the Greek Revival mansion in 1840. It is considered a fine example of ante-bellum architecture, having been designed by Thomas H. Benton, brother of the owner. The brick wings were added much later. The two-story central portion is in Jefferson's classic style. The mansion was in the line of fire during the Battle of Nashville in the Civil War and bears 42 bullet marks.

Melrose. These are the gates to another Greek Revival mansion built in 1836 by Alexander Barrow of Louisiana. It later was occupied by Aaron V. Brown, governor of Tennessee and U.S. Postmaster General.

Glen Leven. This house, located on a North Carolina grant to Thomas Thompson, a signer of the Cumberland Pact, was built in 1857, having been designed by John Thompson. It also was between the lines of the Battle of Nashville, and its walls are scarred by bullets from both sides.

Traveler's Rest. This two-story clapboard plantation house was erected in 1820 by Judge John Overton, who had purchased the land in 1792 and lived there in a log cabin. He was territorial revenue collector and the first lawyer in Nashville, where Andrew Jackson roomed with him. The house now is a museum operated by the Colonial Dames of Tennessee. (Open)

Mayes-Hutton House. Samuel Mayes built this house in 1854 after he sold his slaves in anticipation of emancipation and used the proceeds to pay for the construction. The front doorway forms a trefoil arch and has side-lights and a fan-light. The rooms are large, with high ceilings, and there is a fine curved stairway.

Columbia, Tennessee

Situated on the banks of the Duck River south of Nashville, Columbia is best known as the boyhood home of President James K. Polk and as the one-time greatest street mule market in the world.

It was settled in 1807 and became the county seat the same year. A disastrous flood in 1811, several Indian scares, and a series of earthquakes that lasted several months caused the settlers to consider abandoning the town for a while, but they stayed.

Samuel Polk, father of the President, moved to Columbia from North Carolina in 1807, when the son was eleven years old.

Although the county voted to remain with the Union in 1861, the town became Confederate in sympathy after the fighting broke out. Both Confederate and Union troops occupied the town alternately in 1864 during General Hood's Nashville campaign, but no major engagement took place around Columbia.

The town first became a street mule market in 1840, and thousands of mules and buyers used to congregate there on the first Monday in April of each year. When the demand for mules began to fall off in later years, the enterprising citizens hit on the idea of holding a Mule Day Festival each year as a tourist attraction. Crowds of up to 60,000 people and a parade of 1000 mules with as many as 50 floats and 15 marching bands could be seen on those occasions. The last such festival was held in 1950 after which the encroaching automobile crowded it out.

Samuel Polk House. The father of the President-to-be built this brick house in 1816. James Polk lived there as a boy. It now is a shrine and museum with Polk relics. The downstairs floors are of wide white ash, held together with wooden pegs. Upstairs hand-pinned poplar is used. Samuel Polk was a farmer, surveyor, and land owner. (Open)

Samuel Polk House. Standing on the mantel are a pair of pierced brass vases. The large display case at the right holds a gown made for Mrs. Polk by Worth of Paris while she was mistress of the White House.

Samuel Polk House. This old furniture sits in a parlor that opens from the drawing room through an archway.

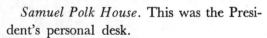

Samuel Polk House. This was the President's personal desk.

Samuel Polk House. This old bed is one of many interesting pieces in the east bedroom.

Two Sisters House. James Walker and his wife, Jane Maria Polk Walker, a daughter of Samuel Polk and brother of James, built this house on land sold or given to them by Samuel Polk in 1816. Later it was sold to Dr. John B. Hays, whose wife, Ophelia, also was a sister of James Polk.

Mercer Hall. This house, built in 1820 by Dr. William Heacock, later was owned by James Polk. In 1829 it was owned by the Reverend James H. Otey, first Protestant Episcopal Bishop in Tennessee, who named it for a friend, Dr. Mercer of Natchez.

Clifton Place. General Gideon J. Pillow built the well-shaded plantation headquarters in 1832. Back of the trees is a portico with four Ionic columns which conceals a gallery with a cast-iron balustrade suspended over the entrance. General Pillow led troops in the Mexican War and was one of the first Tennessee commanders in the Civil War.

Pillow-Bethel House. Jerome Pillow built the Greek Revival mansion in 1845, and it later was the home of his son-in-law, Captain William Bethel. Its large, high-ceiled first-floor rooms open into a broad central hall.

Pope-Spraggins House. Colonel Leroy Pope, who chose the first unpopular name for Huntsville, built this house in 1815. It later became the home of Leroy Pope Walker, who as Confederate Secretary of War gave the order to fire on Fort Sumter. Six massive columns support the roof of the large white dwelling.

Huntsville, Alabama

BEST KNOWN BECAUSE SIX OF ALABAMA'S governors lived there and as the home of Tallulah Bankhead, the actress, Huntsville was settled in 1805 by John Hunt, a veteran of the Revolution from Virginia, who went there on a hunting trip and built a cabin.

Colonel Leroy Pope, a wealthy settler also from Virginia, named the new settlement Twickenham after the home of Alexander Pope, the English poet, but resentment against the British caused the name to be changed in 1811 to honor John Hunt.

Andrew Jackson visited there and bought large tracts of land in the vicinity during the Indian wars.

Huntsville, in the northern part of the state, is where the Constitutional Convention of the Alabama Territory was held in 1819 and where the state government was set up. The town wanted to be the permanent capital of the state but lost out because of its non-central location.

A cotton spinning mill was set up on the nearby Flint River in 1818. It became the terminus of a stagecoach line in 1820 and enjoyed an early prosperity built on cotton and textile mills.

Federal troops captured the town in April, 1862, and destroyed most of its wealth, including railroad shops, warehouses filled with cotton, and business and residential buildings. Railroad tracks and ties were torn up. Postwar recovery was slow.

Howard-Weeden House. This Georgian house, built in 1819, is known for its double walnut doors under a splendid fan-light and for its five carved mantels.

Bibb House. Governor Thomas Bibb built this massive red brick house with its four white Doric columns in 1837, probably for his daughter, Mrs. Joseph Bradley. It is said to have cost more than $30,000.

Fearn-Garth House. This brick house, built in about 1820 by Dr. Thomas Fearn, has a portico of white columns behind the trees to the left.

Erskine-Hendrick House. This rectangular brick house was built in about 1818, and some of its early furniture was hauled from Tennessee by oxen.

Neal House. The 14-room dwelling was built in about 1821 and was the birthplace of John Hunt Morgan, the Confederate general. A half-spiral carved staircase rises from a room at the right of the entrance hall.

Bassett-Young House. Built somewhere between 1819 and 1823, the house has two fan-lighted entrances.

First Presbyterian Church. The congregation of the church with the square tower, built prior to 1860, was organized in 1818.

Tuscaloosa, Alabama

IN 1809, OCCECHEMOLTA, CHIEF OF THE Creek Indians, obtained permission of the government to establish a settlement at the falls of the Warrior River, located about 50 miles southwest of Birmingham. The new settlement became known as Black Warrior Town. But when the Indians revolted against the whites in 1813, General John Coffee's American troops captured and burned the town. Davy Crockett was a member of Coffee's group.

White settlers came in 1816, when Thomas York brought his family and built a cabin. By fall, other settlers came from the Carolinas, Georgia, and Tennessee and, with the aid of slaves, planted corn and cotton. They called their settlement Tuscaloosa.

When the state capital was moved there in 1826, it brought a wave of building of stores and plantation homes, plus steamship service from Mobile.

A female academy was established there in 1829, and the University of Alabama started in 1831.

The moving of the capital to Montgomery in 1846 abruptly stopped the growth and blunted the prosperity of the town, and many business and professional men moved away.

In April, 1865, Federal troops under General Croxton captured the town after a brief skirmish with university cadets, and many of the university buildings were burned.

Gorgas House. One of the university buildings spared by the Federal troops was Gorgas House, built in 1829. The brick dwelling is designed in southern raised plantation style, with two front entrances—one on the first floor, another on the second. Dr. Joseph Gorgas occupied the house when he was president of the university. It now is a splendidly furnished museum, owned by the university. (Open)

Gorgas House. The parlor is tastefully
furnished with period pieces.

Gorgas House. Every older home once
had a what-not on which to display nick-
nacks and *objets d'art*.

Gorgas House. The large wardrobe is delicately carved and has a mirror between its doors.

Gorgas House. This old washstand, fully equipped, is located in a bedroom.

President's Mansion. Charles Nichols of Philadelphia designed the handsome stuccoed brick and sandstone mansion which was completed in 1840. A double winding stairway leads to the front entrance from the ground level. A great central hall is flanked by rooms with deeply recessed windows. The wife of the president of the university who occupied the house then, as now, persuaded Federal troops to spare the building after a blaze had been started in 1865, and the fire then was extinguished by servants.

Jemison House (Cherokee). The Italianate villa with its ornate cupola was designed by a Philadelphia architect and built in the late 1850's by Robert Jemison, who became a Senator in the Confederate Congress. It now is a public library. (Open)

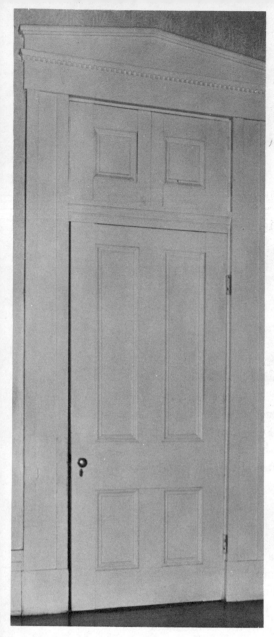

Jemison House. Handsome carving is seen in the entrance hall.

Jemison House. The massive carved newel post, the wainscoting, and the paneling of the stair wall are among the good features of the house.

Jemison House. This marble mantel is located in what had been the drawing room.

Moody House. Now a commercial establishment, the dwelling was built in about 1820. Double doors give access to balconies with wrought-iron balusters. (Open)

Wilson House. This aging structure, built of brick covered with stucco, was erected in about 1826 to serve as a tavern. The first legislative session held after Tuscaloosa became the state capital is said to have convened in a first-floor room of the hostelry.

Seibels House. The brick house cover with white plaster was started in 1845 a Mr. Swann but was not completed un 1855, after it came into the possession Colonel John J. Seibels of South Caroli U.S. Minister to Belgium. It has carv mantels of Italian marble.

Montgomery, Alabama

Named for General Richard Montgomery of Revolutionary fame, the town on the Alabama River near the center of the state was the first capital of the Confederacy.

It is built on the site of early Indian towns, named Ikanatchati and Towasa. James McQueen, a Scot trader, lived there in 1716. Not until 1814 did Arthur Moore and others come and build cabins.

After Alabama lands were offered for sale in 1817, a company of Georgians led by General John Scott built a town there called Alabama, then abandoned it, and built East Alabama nearby. After eastern speculators founded a town called Philadelphia in the vicinity, bitter rivalry ensued and terminated only when the towns were merged as Montgomery in 1819.

The first steamboat from Mobile came in 1821, and a stage line to the east also was established in that year. Lafayette came in 1825, and a guard of honor composed of 300 men escorted him into town. He attended a ball at Freenet's Tavern.

The state capital was moved to Montgomery from Tuscaloosa in 1847. Jefferson Davis was elected president of the Confederacy there in 1861, and the stars and bars were raised above the state capitol in March.

Federal raiders under General James H. Wilson came in April, 1865, and burned small arms factories, the rolling stock of the railroads, and five steamboats.

First White House of the Confederacy.
This is where President Davis and his
family lived during their brief stay in Montgomery. The house was built in 1852 by
William Sayre from plans prepared by A.
M. Bradley. Just before the Civil War, it
was occupied by Colonel Edward Harrison.
It now is a museum containing relics and
personal belongings of Davis. (Open)

First White House. A portrait of Mrs.
Davis appears above the carved mantel.

First White House. This handsomely carved bookcase stands in the library.

First White House. A small settee rests in front of the four-poster bed.

First White House. Another old bookcase and other period furniture are seen in a parlor.

Evans House. The model for the first state flag of Alabama was cut in a front room of this modest house, built in 1853 by John M. Nowell.

Teague House. Now the home of the chamber of commerce, this charming house was built in 1850. During the war, it became the headquarters of Union General Wilson, who read President Lincoln's Emancipation Proclamation to a throng of people from the porch. (Open)

Lomax House. James J. Gilmer, brother of George R. Gilmer, governor of Georgia, built the house in 1848. Later he deeded it to Reuben C. Shorter, Jr., war-time governor of Alabama. Shorter's widow married Tennent Lomax. The house now is an office building. (Open)

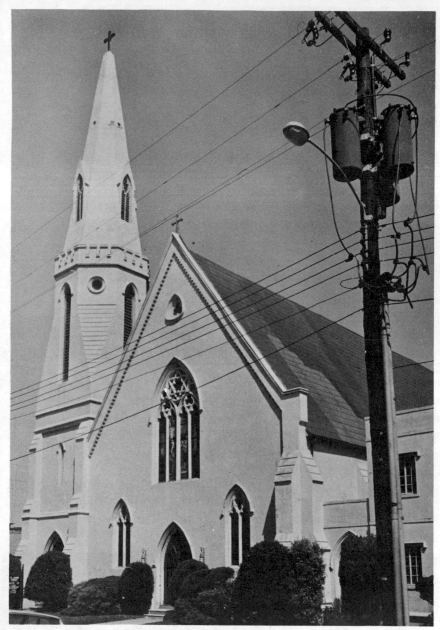

St. John's Church. The brick and stucco church with the conical steeple was erected in 1836. Jefferson Davis is said to have worshipped there. In the nave are 15 memorial windows, six of them in the chancel. Its chimes consist of nine bells. (Open)

Gillman Mansion. This pre-Civil W mansion, quite the finest in town, now is museum. Its Corinthian columns, whi run in front of a large balcony, are flute It was designed by a cousin of Robert Lee and makes generous use of ornament iron in its trim. This mansion was built 1853 by Colonel Edward Watts, and grounds are extensive. (Open)

Selma, Alabama

ALTHOUGH IT WAS VISITED IN 1540 BY Hernando de Soto and in 1702 by the Sieur of Bienville, the first American settlers did not arrive at Selma, situated 50 miles west of Montgomery, until 1809. The first of them was Thomas Moore of Tennessee, who drifted down the Alabama River on a flatboat, built a cabin, and planted corn.

In 1817, three Scotsmen—Robert Lowe, Peter Robinson, and Matthew McLaughlin —built cabins and established a trading center. Initially, they called it High Soapstone Bluff, since the settlement was situated on a bluff above the river.

Also in 1817, a land company was organized by William Rufus King, a U.S. Senator and later vice president, and Dr. George Phillips, a veteran of General Andrew Jackson's army. It was King who renamed the town Selma for the "Song of Selma" by Ossian.

Wealthy cotton planters established large and prosperous plantations nearby. The railroad came in 1848, and in 1850 steamboat traffic on the Alabama River reached its peak.

Selma was a supply depot for the Confederacy during the war, but there was no military action until 1865, when General Wilson reached the city with 9000 men in early April. Under General Nathan Forest, 3000 Confederates put up a desperate defense, but all except Forest and 200 men were trapped and captured.

Morgan House. Built in the 1850's this was the home of General John Tyler Morgan, who was fired on by carpetbaggers while in a second-story room shortly after the war. He later was a U.S. Senator.

Mabry House. The Mabry family which occupied the house for 100 years built the red brick dwelling in 1849.

Burns-Bennett-Bell House. Intricate carving surrounds the entrance and window facings of the house built in 1830. An unsupported spiral staircase rises from the entrance hall. Its workmanship is unusually fine, and it has wide steps and a railing of walnut.

Pettus House. The white frame house, built prior to 1850, is located on grounds that once covered an entire city block. General Edmund Pettus, its owner, entered the Civil War as a private and came out a brigadier general. Later he served as a U.S. Senator for 12 years.

Philpot House. The frame dwelling of the raised cottage type was built in the 1830's. Its owner was killed in the Battle of Selma in 1865.

Plain Gables. A brother of Dr. Hug Bodley, who was shot by gamblers, built t house in 1835. It is best known for an o iron gate and railing that open on t steps leading to its front terrace. The hou located on a high rise with ample ground was damaged by shells during the siege.

Vicksburg, Mississippi

THE SPANISH ESTABLISHED AN OUTPOST here on land obtained from the Indians in 1790 and built a fort the following year. The town that developed is located on bluffs overlooking the Mississippi River north of Natchez.

The Reverend Newitt Vick, a Methodist minister from Virginia, established a mission nearby in 1814 and then bought another tract on which the city now stands. The town was named after him. He started to lay it out but died before the work was well begun. His executor completed the task.

Vicksburg became a flourishing point of export for the state. Wagons pulled by six and eight yokes of oxen hauled bales of cotton there for loading onto river boats. The wagon drivers, gamblers, and other lusty characters gave Vicksburg a bad atmosphere and a worse name in those days.

Admiral Farragut's gunboats bombarded the town in 1862 but withdrew. The armies of Generals Grant and Sherman were repulsed in the same year by the Confederate forces, but in 1863 General Grant finally received the surrender of General John C. Pemberton, owing to hunger, disease, and exposure, after a siege of 47 days.

The era of carpetbagging and reconstruction that followed kept Vicksburg in a state of terror and economic paralysis for the next dozen years, but the carpetbag rule finally was terminated in 1875 and slow recovery began.

Duff Green House. Famous for parties given in its spacious second-floor ballroom in ante-bellum days, the house was built by Dr. Duff Green in the 1840's. It is distinguished by its iron lace-work galleries, front and back. It was a Confederate hospital during the war and now is occupied by the Salvation Army. (Open)

Duff Green House. A once-elegant stairway rises from one side of the hallway in the rear.

Duff Green House. The hand-carved door trim and chair rail still remain in up-stairs rooms.

McNutt House. Alexander McNutt, once governor of Mississippi, built this frame house in about 1826. It is said to be the oldest dwelling in Vicksburg. It has two front doors.

Old Fire House. This structure with its arched doors and bell tower was erected in 1835 for a volunteer fire company composed of young aristocrats.

Warren County Courthouse. The Greek Revival structure built by slave labor is located on one of the highest points in the city. It was begun in 1858 and has four identical façades with fluted Ionic columns. It was designed by William Weldon and constructed by George and Thomas Weldon. (Open)

302

Luckett House. This originally was a one-story house, built in 1830, but the early construction became the upper floor of a two-story dwelling. After the surrender of the city, Federal officers were billeted upstairs and their horses down below.

Willis-Cowan House. This gray painted brick house built in 1840 was the childhood home of Mrs. Junius Ward Johnson, Vicksburg philanthropist. It was the headquarters of General Pemberton.during the siege.

Cedar Grove (Klein Home). When built in 1856, the house stood on spacious grounds with a lawn extending 1500 yards down to the river. The house had a ballroom, banquet room, reception hall, and guest room on the main floor. It now is a museum, with streets and many small houses between it and the river.

Port Gibson, Mississippi

WHEN PASSING THROUGH PORT GIBSON ON his way to Vicksburg, 30 miles to the north, General Grant is said to have stated that "Port Gibson is too beautiful to burn."

The town, located on a curve of Bayou Pierre, was founded in 1788 by Samuel Gibson, a pioneer stockman, bee keeper, orchardist, planter, grist mill owner, and cotton gin operator.

Harman Blennerhassett, associate of Aaron Burr in the Southwest Company, brought his wife to Port Gibson in 1810 after he had been acquitted of charges of treason against the United States.

Irwin Russell, Mississippi's outstanding poet, was born in the cotton town in 1853. It also was the birthplace of Constance Cary, who made the first Confederate flag from "ladies' silk dresses."

Buried there is Resin P. Bowie, designer of the famous Bowie knife first used by his brother, James, in a duel at Natchez and found on James' body when he was killed at the Alamo in 1836.

The Hermitage. This long southern-type plantation house was the birthplace of Confederate General B. G. Humphreys, first post-war governor of Mississippi. It was built in about 1800 by the general's father, George W. Humphreys.

Russell Memorial. Built in the early 1800's, the square white brick house originally was the home of Samuel Gibson, founder of the town. It was a Confederate hospital during the war and was later used by the Port Gibson Female College for 104 years. Then it was converted into a memorial to Irwin Russell, the poet.

Gage House. This house, built in 1851, was the home of James A. Gage, one of 50 older people said to have been taken to Vicksburg as hostages by General Grant.

Gage House. A handsome paneled double entrance door is shaded by the second-floor gallery.

Serenity. This one-story frame house, built in 1817, was the birthplace of flag designer Constance Cary, whose father was a kinsman of Thomas Jefferson. It was from the front porch of this house that General Grant is believed to have made his complimentary remark about Port Gibson.

Presbyterian Church. The steeple of this church, erected in 1829, is surmounted by a large galvanized iron hand instead of a cross. The hand originally was made of wood. The edifice has a slave gallery and a chandelier donated by the owners of the river boat *Robert E. Lee*.

Idlewild. Built in 1833, this tree-shaded plantation house has 12-foot doors and windows.

Idlewild. The old carriage block and low iron gates remain in front of the plantation house.

The Hil. The brick house, now in ruins, was built in the early 1800's by the father of Confederate General Early Van Dorn, who was one of four brigadier generals in the state's army and later commanded the army of the West.

Natchez, Mississippi

OVERLOOKING THE MISSISSIPPI RIVER from a series of high bluffs in the southwest corner of the state, Natchez has been under the flags of France, Spain, England, the Confederacy, and the United States.

Although it is believed that De Soto's men came to the area as early as 1542, and in 1682 the explorers La Salle and Tonti visited there, the town formally came into existence in 1716 when the Frenchman, Bienville, established a fort at the present site of the town. He gave it the name of Fort Rosalie, but the settlement which quickly sprang up around the fort soon took the name of Natchez, after the Indian tribe that lived there.

From the beginning, trouble existed between the settlers and the Indians, and in 1729 the Indians rose in revolt against the French, captured and destroyed Fort Rosalie, and massacred a large part of the population. French forces, aided by Choctaw Indians, waged a punitive war against the Natchez tribe, which resulted in complete defeat of the latter.

In 1763, Great Britain obtained possession of Natchez under a treaty with France. British rule, however, was short, for in 1779 the Spanish captured the city.

In 1798, the Spanish garrison evacuated Natchez, and the Stars and Stripes first flew over Natchez soil. The town became the seat of government for the Territory of Mississippi, which became a state in 1817.

From that date until the outbreak of the Civil War, Natchez epitomized America's golden age of good living, thanks largely to the cotton crop. It was the only large port on the Mississippi River between the mouth of the Ohio River and New Orleans. With the coming of the steamboat, the river trade was accelerated and many were the fortunes made by Natchez citizens. The lavishness of that period is reflected in the ante-bellum town and plantation homes, many of which have been carefully preserved.

After Mississippi seceded from the Union, Natchez was shelled by Federal gunboats but little damage was done. The war, however, destroyed the fortunes of the citizens, and the town witnessed a decline that lasted until shortly before World War II.

D'Evereaux. William St. John Elliott, a close friend of Henry Clay, built this charming mansion in 1840 and named it after his mother's family. Its double drawing rooms originally furnished in rosewood have magnificent chandeliers. It was constructed on a wooded site of 12 acres and has an elaborate terraced garden in the rear. The mansion has beautiful fluted two-story Doric columns and galleries in both front and rear. This view was made from the garden. (Open)

D'Evereaux. Fine old furniture graces the tastefully decorated double drawing room.

D'Evereaux. The dining table is set with
old family possessions for an Easter dinner.

D'Evereaux. This attractive cornice runs
around the entrance hall.

D'Evereaux. The imported chandelier hangs from an attractive medallion in a parlor.

Stanton Hall. This mansion was completed in 1857 by Frederick Stanton, an Irish gentleman who became a wealthy cotton broker. Some of the ceilings are 22 feet high. It has mahogany doors, Carrara marble mantels, and gigantic mirrors which were imported from Europe.

Cherokee. Started in 1794, this was the home of Alvarez Fisk, a wealthy cotton broker and philanthropist of the 1830's and 1840's. It has an interesting cross hall and graceful winding stairs. (Open)

Connelly's Tavern. The old frame hostelry is situated on a steep terraced hill. It was built in 1795 during the Spanish rule and overlooks the esplanade. The lower floor was paved with brick. It is regarded as a noble example of Spanish provincial architecture. The tavern has low ceilings but several rooms are vaulted. (Open)

Bontura. The L-shaped dwelling was built in 1832. The galleries across its narrow front are ornamented with delicate lace ironwork. (Open)

First Presbyterian Church. Lewis Weeks of Boston designed the stuccoed brick church erected in 1829. Its pews had wooden doors, and there is a slave gallery. (Open)

Mercer House. This house, built in 1818, is distinguished principally by the fact that Andrew Jackson stayed here and made a speech from the front porch in 1840.

Old Spanish House. Typical of old Spanish town dwellings, this house was built in 1796 or earlier. It has outside stairways and a kitchen attached by a hyphen.

Metcalfe House. Peter Little, a pioneer lumberman, built this house in 1849 and is said to have deeded it to a church on condition that the frequent entertaining of preachers in his house would stop.

Rosalie. The square, red brick Georgian mansion was built in the early 1800's by Peter Little, the lumberman. It has four Tuscan columns across the pedimented front façade. Its parlors are 21 feet square, and it has five-foot windows, 14-foot ceilings, and seven-foot mantels. General Grant and his family spent several days there in 1863 when the mansion served as a Union headquarters. (Open)

Rosalie. Over the front door is a fan-light
and interesting ceiling decoration.

Rosalie. The marble mantel and large
oval mirror provide a background for the
stunning banquet table with its old silver.

Rosalie. Back of the crystal chandelier, which was imported from France and hangs from a medallion, is seen an elaborate cornice.

Rosalie. The Italian marble mantel under the large mirror is in the double parlor which contains a complete set of rosewood furniture.

Green Leaves. The Greek Revival dwelling of 14 rooms was built prior to 1812. It is of raised brick and frame construction with a narrow classic portico and has a detached brick kitchen. (Open)

The Elms. This house with its long galleries was built in about 1785, probably by Spanish Governor Pedro Piernas. Its low ceilings, narrow window facings, large chimneys, and heavy hand-made iron hinges indicate its Spanish origin. (Open)

Dunleith. General Charles Dahlgren built this square mansion in 1847. Its tall Doric columns are surrounded by galleries with delicate wrought-iron railings.

Auburn. Levi Weeks of Boston designed this house built in 1812 by Judge Lyman G. Harding, first attorney general of the Territory and of the state of Mississippi. It has an imposing entrance door with a canopied, fan-lighted transom, which is repeated on the balcony above, and an outstanding spiral staircase. The mansion now stands in a city park.

Natchitoches, Louisiana

PRONOUNCED "NAKATISH" LOCALLY, THIS is the oldest permanent settlement in Louisiana. It was established in about 1714 as a French trading post known as Fort St. Jean Baptiste, then took its Indian name later.

It is located about 55 miles northwest of Alexandria on the west bank of Cane River Lake, which formerly was the main channel of the Red River.

The area was first explored by La Salle in 1687 and then was settled in 1691 by Canary Islanders. Juchereau de St. Denis was sent by the French to establish trade relations with Spain and with Mexico and left troops there in 1713. They were besieged by Natchez Indians for 22 days in 1732, but the Indians finally were annihilated by St. Denis. U.S. troops took over in 1804.

The first building was put up in about 1759 when Jean Baptiste Prudhomme built a one-story residence that became a tavern. It was torn down in 1937.

A change of course in the Red River left the once promising trading community bereft of transportation advantages in 1832.

Williams (Tauzin) House. This long, low plantation house was erected in 1776 on the site of an Indian trading post. The walls are made of adobe mixed with deer hair. The sills and rafters of cypress are held together with wooden pins. The windows once had iron bars for protection against Indians.

Williams House. The old chest and grandfather clock stand in front of a wood-paneled wall in the parlor.

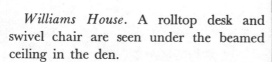

Williams House. A rolltop desk and swivel chair are seen under the beamed ceiling in the den.

Williams House. A secretary and two early portraits are seen against another wall of the parlor.

Tauzin (Campbell) House. Joseph Tauzin built this house in about 1840, to replace one built on the same site in 1792, for his bride, Marie Chamard, whose ten children were born there.

Lauve House. This raised plantation cottage was constructed in 1806 by Nicholas Lauve. French windows open onto a wide gallery. Theophile Tauzin, Jr., bought the house in 1836 from C. Pavie.

Hughes and Lacoste Buildings. The former structure, on the left, put up by Gabriel Prudhomme in 1853 has a second-floor gallery in the rear. He is said to have chartered a ship to bring the building materials from Europe. The iron shutters are believed to have stopped the fire that destroyed buildings to the south. Thomas Lacoste in 1852 built the building to the right, which once housed the Comus Club. Its cast-iron grillwork was imported from France. It was used for balls and other social functions.

House of Brides. This house was built in about 1790 as part of the dowry for a daughter of the Bruard family, who was marrying a Prudhomme. A parlor in which many marriages have been performed has a rose, blue, and green bas-relief medallion.

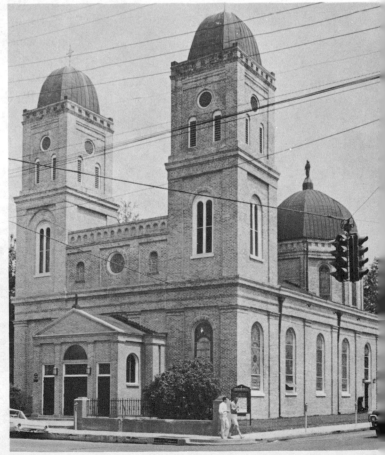

Church of the Immaculate Conception. First known as St. Francis Cathedral, the church was built in 1838. The twin gray brick towers are topped by octagonal domes. (Open)

Serdot Prudhomme House. This house was built in 1850 for Tante Huppe as a gift from her brother after the death of her third husband. Each room has an outside entrance.

Leopold Levy House. The first floor of this building put up in the early 1800's is made of brick, the second floor of wood. It originally was an office building occupied by Trescini and Soldini. The balcony added just before the Civil War has an ornate cast-iron railing.

Sullivan House. This is the pre-Civil War home of Miss Mary Campbell, who is said to have rejected the suit of General U. S. Grant when he was stationed there in the 1830's.

Eden Plantation House. This one and a half-story frame house was built before the Civil War by Benjamin Kitchen Hunter.

Alexandria, Louisiana

SITTING ON THE BANK OF THE RED RIVER and once called "Les Rapides," Alexandria was almost destroyed by fire in 1864 during the Civil War, so there are no important older buildings left inside the town, although there are numerous plantation houses close by.

The town was settled sometime during the 1760's, although the Spanish erected a stockade and trading post there shortly after 1714.

It was laid out in 1810 in the center of the state by Alexander Fulton, a wealthy land owner and merchant, and named after his daughter.

In 1819, a school called College of Rapides was established there on land donated by John Casson. A bank was opened in 1824.

It became a shipping and trading center on the Red River with large plantations devoted to cotton, sugar cane, and other crops; then lumbering assumed importance.

The first railroad west of the Mississippi River, begun by planter Ralph Smith-Smith, was 40 miles long and hauled cotton and cane from plantations to steamboats on the river in the Alexandria area.

The town was occupied by Federal troops during the Civil War. There was almost no bloodshed, but the troops fired the town after being defeated in the Battle of Mansfield.

Tyrone Plantation House. This pre-war house once belonged to General Sprague of New Orleans and later to General Mason Graham. General William T. Sherman was a frequent guest there before the Civil War.

Kent Plantation House. Pierre Baillo built the raised plantation house in the late 1700's. It contained fine woodwork and elaborate fireplaces. The wings were added later. It finally became the headquarters of an American Legion Post and then was cut in half and moved.

Inglewood Plantation House. Surrounded by galleries with slender white pillars, this house was completed in 1838. Its wings have galleries on three sides.

Inglewood. An intricate plaster cornice and ceiling decoration adorn the living room.

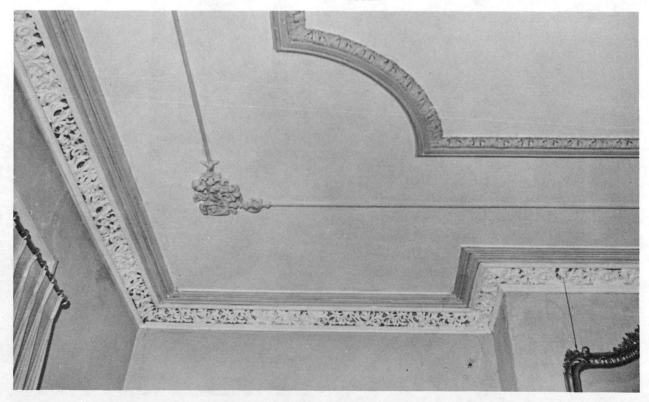

Inglewood. This four-poster bed has a fringed top and handsome spread and quilt.

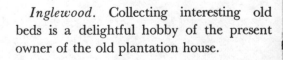
Inglewood. Collecting interesting old beds is a delightful hobby of the present owner of the old plantation house.

Inglewood. Elaborate carving enhances the appeal of this unusual bed.

Rosalie Plantation House. This long, low, attractive house, completed in 1838, was built by Gervais Baillo, son of Pierre who built Kent. It has a brick smokehouse.

St. Martinville, Louisiana

LOCATED ON THE GLAMOROUS BAYOU Teche, the town once was known as Le Petit Paris.

The first settler probably was Gabriel Fuselier de la Claire, who purchased a tract from Rinemo, an Indian chief, in 1760. By 1764, the Marquis de Vaugine had established an indigo plantation nearby.

After the Spanish occupation in 1769, the settlement became a military outpost named Poste de Attakapas for an Indian tribe.

Its first prosperity was based on indigo and a smuggling trade with the British by way of the Atchafalaya and Vermillion Rivers.

The town was incorporated as St. Martinville in 1812, shortly after Louisiana became a state. It was named in honor of the fourth-century French bishop, Martin.

In rapid succession, beginning about 1855, a series of catastrophes, including fire, an epidemic of yellow fever, a hurricane, the passing of the steamboat era, and the Civil War brought a decline to the town's early glory.

St. John Plantation House. Alexandre Etienne de Clouet, son of an early commandant of the Poste des Attakapas, built the plantation house in about 1828. It has high ceilings, large doors and windows, and a huge dining room.

Acadian House. This galleried cottage with its outside staircase is supposed to have sheltered Louis Arcenaux, the Gabriel of Longfellow's "Evangeline." It was built in the 1700's by the widow of the Chevalier de la Houssaye and has been furnished with relics and primitive pieces from the vicinity. There are no doors between the upstairs bedrooms; all must be entered from the gallery. (Open)

Acadian House. A primitive wooden plow, a deerskin rug, and a unique chair made from the horns of oxen are among the curiosities on view in the house.

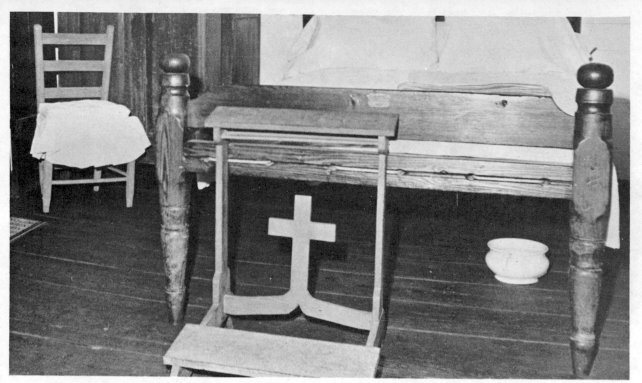

Acadian House. A prayer stool rests at the end of the bed with its rope springs.

Acadian House. A simple four-poster, a cradle, a washstand, and a small bathtub are seen under the beams in a second-floor bedroom.

Acadian House. Among the many relics are the coats-of-arms of early Louisiana families.

St. Martinville Catholic Church. The gray cement-covered brick church was erected in 1832, although a part may have been in existence in 1795. Above the altar is an old painting of the town's patron saint—St. Martin and the Beggar. (Open)

Parish Courthouse. The narrow Greek Revival building was erected with slave labor in 1853, although the wings were added later. It contains records dating back to 1760. (Open)

Olde Labbe House. Once a raised platform plantation house, but now resting on the ground, the dwelling was built in the early 1800's. It has a curved stairway of stained cypress.

Beauregard. Believed to have been built in the 1830's, the house once was owned by Judge René Beauregard, son of the famous Confederate general. It was altered in the 1850's and 1860's and has recently been restored. It now is situated in Chalmette National Historical Park. The plastered brick walls are apricot in color, and the eight white columns made of brick and plastered in white. (Open)

New Orleans, Louisiana

FRANCE AND SPAIN RULED NEW ORLEANS for nearly 100 years before it became part of the United States. The old part of town, known as the Vieux Carré or French Quarter, is distinguished by its narrow streets, quaint architecture, ironwork, and courtyards.

Located on a sharp bend in the Mississippi River above the Gulf of Mexico, New Orleans was founded in about 1718 by Jean Baptiste LeMoyne, Sieur de Bienville. It was named in honor of the Duc d'Orleans, Regent of France, and became the capital of the great French colonial empire in 1723, succeeding Biloxi.

Then, following the partitioning of the territory between Spain and England, the town became the capital of Spanish Louisiana in 1763.

Old New Orleans was almost completely destroyed by fire in 1788 when more than 800 buildings were razed. Then, in 1794, another 212 were lost in another conflagration.

The Americans came soon after the colony was sold to the United States in 1803. At the close of the War of 1812, New Orleans was belatedly attacked by British forces under General Sir Edward Pakenham, but American forces under General Andrew Jackson defeated the invaders in January, 1815.

In the Civil War, New Orleans was the chief port of the Confederacy and became an early target for Union forces. Admiral David G. Farragut came up the Mississippi River with 44 ships in 1862 and crippled two defending forts in a five-day bombardment, after which New Orleans was forced to surrender. Reconstruction after the war was a slow and painful experience, and civilian rule was not restored until 1877.

NEARBY PLANTATION HOUSES

Beauregard. The narrow stairway with its curved railing winds up from the end of the hallway.

Lebeau. F. B. Lebeau erected this large plantation house in 1850. It is built of brick with a covering of wood for protection from moisture. Its railings contain unusual ironwork, and its octagonal cupola had a fine view of the Mississippi River.

Derbigny. This little plantation house, built in the 1820's, originally was situated in an orange and pecan grove.

Magnolia Lane. Edward Fortier built this plantation house in 1814 on a Spanish grant. It is where Francis Quinette grew the first strawberries in Louisiana.

Seven Oaks. The square plantation house, now empty, was built in 1830 by the widow of Michael Zeringue. It has 18 rooms and is completely surrounded by wide upper and lower galleries that are supported by 30 Doric columns.

Elmwood. This plantation house, constructed about 1762, was badly damaged by fire in 1940, but the pillars survived and were incorporated into the restored structure. It was built by La Frenière, who came over from France with Iberville and Bienville. W. C. Claiborne, first U.S. governor of Louisiana, is believed to have lived there. The house now is a restaurant. (Open)

Whitehall. Built in the 1850's by Francois Pascalise de Labarre, this plantation house later became a gambling hall, then a Jesuit retreat, and now is a private school. Federal troops camped there during the war. (Open)

FRENCH QUARTER

Ursiline Convent. This, the first nunnery Louisiana, was completed in 1734. It ay be the oldest building in the Mississi-pi Valley.

Lafitte Blacksmith Shop. Built prior to 1771, this old house is said to have been used by the Lafitte brothers—Jean and Pierre—as a blacksmith shop to make them appear innocent and respectable citizens while engaged in their nefarious smuggling and piracy. Hand-hewn diagonal timbers are seen within the brickwork in the outer walls.

St. Louis Cathedral. The edifice was completed in 1794 with funds provided by Don Almonester, on condition that mass be said for the repose of his soul every Saturday. (Open)

The Cabildo. Built in 1795, this was the old seat of Spanish rule and was the scene of the transfer of Louisiana from France to the United States. It now is a museum. (Open)

Montegut House. This old house was built prior to 1799. It has a spacious courtyard in the rear and wrought-iron framework guarding its front windows.

Labranche Building. Jean Baptiste Labranche, a well-to-do sugar planter, built
this three-story structure in the early 1830's.
Its ironwork is outstanding.

Gayarre Home. This house was built
some time before 1777 and was the home
of Charles Gayarre, famed Louisiana lawyer and historian.

Casa Flinard. Gerome Flinard, first owner of the house, was a Spanish Grandee. Built in about 1800, it has hand-hewn cypress timbers in its floors and ceilings, a carved walnut staircase, and beautiful mantels.

Miro House. This house dates back almost to 1790 and may have been the home of Don Estevan Miro, Spanish governor from 1785 to 1791.

Spanish Comandancia. This house was occupied as early as 1774, but historians disbelieve the story that Spanish mounted police were stationed there. It became a market place for fish oil.

Lafitte Bank. Jean Louis Chesneau built the house in 1800. It became a bank at the beginning of the Civil War. The bank was owned by Lafitte and Dufilho.

348

Patio Royal. Built about 1801 as a private residence, this house became the Bank of Louisiana and later was the home of Paul Morphy, the celebrated chess king.

The Roquette House. Handsome wrought-iron brackets support the balcony of this house built in the early 1800's and occupied at one time by Dominique Roquette, a wine merchant.

Lanusse House. This house with the splendid wrought iron was erected during the Spanish era by Pablo Lanusse.

Bibliography

Cooper, J. Wesley. *A Treasure of Louisiana Plantation Homes,* 1961.

———. *Natchez, A Treasure of Ante-Bellum Homes,* 1958.

The Garden Club of Virginia. *Homes and Gardens in Old Virginia,* 1962.

Hammond, Ralph. *Ante-Bellum Mansions of Alabama,* 1951.

Lynn, Stuart M. *New Orleans,* 1949.

Perkerson, Medora F. *White Columns in Georgia,* 1952.

Pratt, Dorothy, and Richard. *A Guide to Early American Homes—South,* 1956.

Rothery, Agnes. *Houses Virginians Have Loved,* 1954.

Sullivan, John T. *Madison County (Kentucky) Past and Present,* 1965.

Thomas, Elizabeth Patterson. *Old Kentucky Homes and Gardens,* 1939.